ALTERNATIVES TO THE PEACE CORPS

*A Directory of Third World
and US Volunteer Opportunities*

Ninth Edition

EDITED BY JOAN POWELL

FOOD FIRST BOOKS

OAKLAND, CALIFORNIA

NINTH EDITION, 2000

COVER AND TEXT DESIGN BY COLORED HORSE STUDIOS

TYPESET IN DEMOCRATICA AND PERPETUA TYPEFACES,
WITH LAUREAT ORNAMENTS

COVER PHOTO FROM CORBIS IMAGES, COPYRIGHT ©2000 CORBIS

Library of Congress Catalog-in-Publication-Data

Alternatives to the Peace Corps: a directory of Third World and US volunteer opportunities/edited by Joan Powell.—9th ed.

    p.cm.

  Includes bibliographical references and index.

  ISBN 0935028-83-8

  1. Voluntarism—Directories. 2. Community development—Directories.

  I. Powell, Joan.

  HM49.V64 A47 2000
  361.3'7025—dc21   00-045602

Food First Books are distributed by:
LPC Group
1436 West Randolph Street
Chicago, IL 60607
(800) 243-0138
www.coolbooks.com

Printed in Canada
10 9 8 7 6 5 4 3 2 1

FOR LAND & LIBERTY
JOBS & JUSTICE

TABLE Of CONTENTS

ACKNOWLEDGEMENTS

Alternatives to the Peace Corps is published in response to the numerous inquiries Food First receives from individuals seeking opportunities to gain community development experience.

Becky Buell, a staff member at Food First from 1985 to 1988, researched and wrote the original edition in 1986 with the assistance of Kari Hamerschlag, a Food First intern. Tremendous demand for the booklet created a continuing need to revise and update it periodically.

Joan Powell revised the introduction and updated and expanded the listings of volunteer opportunities for this ninth edition.

This book is made possible by the volunteers and friends who provide updates and additions each year. Many thanks go to the returned Peace Corps volunteers who have offered their perspectives in the development of this guide.

FOREWORD

International volunteering is one of the more positive aspects
of the globalization of our economies, cultures, and social
and political structures. In trade pacts and common markets,
through the consolidation of capital by a handful of multina-
tional corporations, the diverse peoples and nations of the
world are becoming more and more mutually dependent; the
"worldwide web" is an apt description of more than just our
Internet connections. Volunteering is widely viewed as a way
to effect development and promote justice in troubled areas of
the world, and the number, stature, and influence of volunteer-
based organizations has increased markedly over the last decade.
Under the auspices of numerous governmental and nongovernmental organizations (NGOs), countless individuals have
volunteered their time and resources to bring about social
change. The UN has designated 2001 the Year of the Volunteer
in recognition of the importance of voluntary action.

The Cold War ushered in a special kind of international
development aid that was also a battle for the minds and
loyalties of emerging nations. Established by President Kennedy
in 1961, the Peace Corps was intended to serve as a public
relations tool to counter Soviet influence and, indeed, it was
perceived as a form of benevolent foreign aid with a young
American face. Thousands of Americans have worked abroad
through the Peace Corps since then, bringing home valuable
experiences of foreign countries and the inner workings of
government-sponsored aid.

Since the Kennedy era, a generation of Americans has grown
up supporting civil rights at home and seeking change in
American foreign policy in Vietnam, El Salvador, South Africa,

and a host of other countries. Many believe that US foreign policy has not always been helpful in building more equitable societies in the Third World. Neither human rights nor sustainable development has been the first priority of government foreign aid.

At the Institute for Food and Development Policy/Food First, we have researched world hunger extensively. Our analyses have led us to conclude that hunger is not caused by scarcity of food or poor people's lack of know-how or even overpopulation, it is caused by an unequal system of food production and distribution that enriches a small segment of society. Because of these inequalities, we emphasize the role of volunteers as participants in social change that is designed by and for local people.

Food First published the first edition of *Alternatives to the Peace Corps* in 1986 as a response to frequent requests for guidance on international volunteer opportunities that had no or minimal government strings attached. *Alternatives to the Peace Corps* was the first guide of its kind that offered options for voluntary service with private agencies that emphasized social change. The agencies and programs listed here are sensitive to the need for volunteers who are willing to learn about the local culture and support efforts by local grassroots organizations.

Another important priority in publishing *Alternatives to the Peace Corps* is to place volunteers with agencies working for social and political reform in the United States. Hunger and poverty is not just a foreign problem; here at home one in five children are growing up in poverty. The gap between rich and poor is increasing, creating a large underclass. Americans have always had a tradition of volunteer work; volunteerism has supported many of our community-based organizations, from parent-school groups and the YMCA/YWCA to coalitions against homelessness. Dedicated volunteers for self-help initiatives are needed more than ever today to counteract government cuts in programs for the disadvantaged, the elderly, immigrants, and the poor.

This ninth edition of *Alternatives to the Peace Corps* is dedicated to those fine men and women who want to share their talents with humanity to make this a better world.

WHY VOLUNTEER?

BEFORE MAKING A commitment, it is important to clarify your motives. You may be drawn to voluntary service by a desire to help people striving for social, political, or economic change; you may be interested in learning about another culture and society; you may be eager to gain experience that will help you find employment. Your motivation may consist of all these reasons and more besides, but thoroughly understanding why you wish to volunteer can help keep you focused and confident during your service, and ensure that you get the most from the experience.

Humanitarian motivations lead many prospective volunteers to communities plagued by extreme poverty and injustice. A volunteer may wish to feed the hungry, heal the sick, or house the homeless, but these social and political problems are often more complex than they initially seem. Learning the dynamics of a community is the greatest challenge to a volunteer, making the volunteer's most appropriate role that of a student. Working for justice can better your understanding of the forces that keep people impoverished and of politics at the local, national, and international levels. For many, volunteer experience is the beginning of a lifelong commitment to ending poverty and hunger. This resource guide provides a list of some of the groups that work to support development as defined by local people.

Another motivation for voluntary service is the desire to learn more about other societies. Living in another country can build your appreciation of the richness of other cultures and enable you to gain comparative perspective on life in the United States. Apart from formal long term volunteering, work brigades, study tours, and international education programs offer short term exposure and, often, a component of historical and theoretical insight into problems faced by the communities you visit. Many such programs are specifically designed for students. In this resource guide, a number of tour, education, and shorter-term programs are also listed.

If your concern is to improve your qualifications for a career in development, an unconventional work experience may enhance your candidacy. The best programs place volunteers with local nongovernmental organizations (NGOs) that have requested a volunteer for a specific purpose. In these circumstances, volunteers have a better chance of making a meaningful contribution. These placements often require some skills—computer, teaching, agriculture, appropriate technology, health care, or fundraising. It would be wise to develop specific technical skills as well as language competency that may be of use to an organization.

Concerned American citizens who want to help impoverished people don't need to travel around the globe to fulfill their goals. The challenges of community development here at home are immense. For this reason, one section of this resource guide is dedicated to US organizations. Voluntary service in low income communities in the US can also be a valuable educational experience or preparation for future work. By advocating for policies that are more accountable to the poor, we can help create a political climate in which grassroots efforts can flourish both here and abroad. Work in developing nations can deepen our understanding of these tasks and make our work at home more effective.

There are inappropriate reasons for wanting to volunteer abroad, two of which deserve a brief mention because both pose easy temptations. Simple escapism—the desire to get away from home to evade personal problems or because you can't decide on a career—is an understandable impulse, but not the best motivation for volunteering. If you are troubled, preoccupied, or at loose ends, your effectiveness overseas will be diminished. The other ill-advised reason might be called crusaderism, and is almost the reverse: wanting to travel to far-flung pockets of deprivation and change everything in the space of three months. To expect too much is to set yourself up for disappointment. We might do well to heed the observation of Dorothy Day, co-founder of the Catholic Worker Movement in the 1930s, who cited the life of Jesus in her own assessment of the slow pace of social change: "What we do is so little that we may seem to be constantly failing—but then, so did He; He met with apparent failure on the Cross...unless the seed fall into the earth and die, there is not a harvest. And why must we see the results of our giving? Our work is to sow—another generation will be reaping the harvest."

LESSONS FROM
THE PEACE CORPS

DECIDING TO VOLUNTEER is a difficult decision. Knowing why you want to volunteer is the first step toward choosing among the many varied options of where to go, with what organization, and with what funds. A common solution to this dilemma is to choose a government-sponsored volunteer program such as the Peace Corps of the United States in which all expenses are paid, and training, health and accident insurance, travel expenses, and even a stipend are provided. Serving with a government agency may also seem inherently safer than traveling thousands of miles from home under the auspices of a tiny NGO. The Peace Corps name commands a level of recognition and respect that less well-known groups are hard-pressed to match.

This solution seems simple enough. But the Peace Corps and programs like it are not always as straightforward as they seem. The choice of countries in which an agency works, the projects it supports, and the role of its volunteers have many political, social, and cultural implications. Volunteers are more than well-meaning individuals. They are representatives of the organizations that sponsor them. As such, volunteers are expected to communicate the governmental, religious, or institutional values and objectives of the organization they represent.

For example, the Peace Corps, the most well-known voluntary service organization, is an agency of the US government. The Peace Corps volunteer is part of the national team dispatched by the US State Department and accountable to the

US ambassador in the host country. The Peace Corps is inevitably linked to US foreign policy objectives, as is the Peace Corps volunteer.

The Peace Corps was founded by President John F. Kennedy to build America's positive image at home and overseas. Ostensibly an apolitical organization, its image was tainted from the outset by underlying foreign policy manipulations. One initial goal of the Peace Corps was to counter Soviet cultural and political influence in the Third World. A 1962 National Security Action Memorandum signed by Kennedy ordered the directors of the CIA, USAID, and Peace Corps to "give utmost attention and emphasis to programs designed to counter Communist indirect aggression [through]...support of local police forces for internal security and counter-insurgency purposes." Prodded by a Senate committee investigating intelligence agencies in 1977, the CIA reported that it had not used the Peace Corps as cover for its operations since 1975. The assertion may have been intended as reassurance, but it raises concerns about what those operations were and whether similar maneuvers continue today under a different dispensation. US military and counterintelligence assistance to numerous governments over the last several decades (most recently and notably in Colombia) has perpetuated economic disparities and human rights abuses, and hindered development for poor communities.

The ideological underpinnings of the Peace Corps have altered to reflect the changing nature and objectives of US foreign policy. With the end of the Cold War, the Peace Corps has evolved to fit the new character of international relations. Over the last decade the US government clearly defined the battle lines in the Third World in economic terms. By influencing the patterns of resource control, legislation, and monetary policy within developing countries, whether through International

Monetary Fund (IMF)-imposed structural adjustment programs or free trade agreements, the US government has found new ways to keep the Third World safe for its brand of capitalism. By the 1990s, US policy was no longer defined primarily by military influence, but by its ability to mold societies through economic intervention.

The Peace Corps fits neatly into this new form of intervention in the Third World. Under the leadership of director Loret Miller Ruppe during the Reagan administration, the Peace Corps began billing itself less as a symbol of good will and more seriously as a development agency. Through initiatives such as the African Food System Initiative and the Small Enterprise Development Program, Peace Corps volunteers began promoting private enterprise and the development of export production in the rural sector. The development of these programs coincided with the IMF's structural adjustment programs, which forced Third World governments to cut price supports for production of basic grains. Economic policies handed down from IMF and the World Bank have pushed poor farmers away from growing basic food crops and toward planting specialty crops for foreign markets, which is economically risky, environmentally unsound, and often results in farmers losing their land. The net impact of these changes eroded the standing of poor farmers. Many impoverished countries now import basic grains and legumes and small farmers find themselves carrying debt as they move into export production.

In 1992 the Peace Corps began establishing a presence in the Republics of the former Soviet Union and Eastern Europe. The goal of this program is to support small business development and privatization of state-controlled economies. Volunteers included economists, accountants, bankers, and specialists in advertising, marketing, business planning, management, and privatization. Observers noted that the Peace Corps was now "fulfilling the goal of having Americans help transform the communist states into capitalist democracies." Former Peace Corps director Elaine L. Chao saw this move as putting the Peace Corps on "freedom's new frontier." As the 1990s wore on, however, the Russian economy—along with those of other Eastern European states—foundered badly under US-advised "shock therapy" conversion to capitalism, with thousands thrown out of work, many workers going unpaid, and vast increases in wealth inequality. The Peace Corps, like the rest of the government, showed little inclination in word or deed to qualify its devotion to free markets in the former Soviet Union; today, the often high-profile programs in Eastern Europe continue.

The objection may be raised that the Peace Corps simply goes where it is invited, and does what it is asked to do. That's true, up to a point. But the projects the agency is willing to engage in and the numbers of volunteers it is willing to send— both with an eye to geopolitical interest—also enter into the equation. Also, bear in mind that foreign governments, not grassroots organizations, submit the requests for volunteers, and there is no guarantee that they have their citizens' best interests at heart. It is perhaps telling—and somewhat ironic— that two Peace Corps initiatives announced in the past few years are assistance with host nation NGO development and with the formation of host countries' own volunteer programs. If the Peace Corps is serious about its goal of capacity-building (in development lingo, imparting skills and knowledge rather than simply performing charity), then in these two cases it may assist host nations right out of their need for the Peace Corps. This should not be considered a bad thing.

OTHER LESSONS FROM
GOVERNMENT-BASED
DEVELOPMENT AID

A LOOK AT some of the other federal agencies involved in development work is in order. The US Agency for International Development (USAID), also created by Kennedy in 1961, states frankly on its website that it "conducts foreign assistance and humanitarian aid to advance the political and economic interests of the United States." Through field offices in foreign countries, USAID funnels monetary aid and technical assistance to projects in keeping with the purposes of US foreign policy. Some of these projects have involved leaning on governments to privatize state-owned industries, to allow greater foreign investment, and to decrease spending on social programs such as health, education, and food subsidies. USAID has helped to uphold the regime of debt service imposed upon many poor countries by the IMF and World Bank, as described above, and to enforce the claims of US corporations conducting business abroad. Too often, the agency has pushed for costly solutions to local problems, and its projects have enriched only the wealthiest citizens of developing nations. In this guide, we have tried to avoid listing organizations that accept money from USAID.

Another government volunteer service program offers an instructive partial contrast to the Peace Corps. Volunteers In Service To America (VISTA), created by President Johnson in 1964 as the "domestic Peace Corps," retains as its purpose development work in poor communities in the United States, addressing such issues as homelessness, illiteracy, and economic and neighborhood revitalization. As with the Peace Corps,

volunteers are prohibited from engaging in political activity
during their participation, and there can be little doubt that the
stated aims of the projects VISTA supports seldom run counter
to official US policy on poverty. For example, in the last few
years VISTA has assisted in the implementation and support of
welfare reform legislation. Yet VISTA's emphasis on community
organizing and self-help over service delivery—as well as its
removal from the realm of foreign relations and the imperative
of upholding our image overseas—garnered the agency a repu-
tation for activism, even radicalism, in its early years. Under
subsequent conservative administrations, VISTA gradually
shifted its focus away from remedying poverty and toward more
general service endeavors; it promoted volunteerism less as an
agent of social change and more as a salutary and fulfilling activity for concerned citizens. President Clinton continued the
trend, signing in 1993 the National and Community Service
Trust Act which subsumed VISTA under the newly created
Corporation for National Service, or AmeriCorps. The purpose
of AmeriCorps is, as one commentator said of the later VISTA,
"to mobilize volunteers, not the poor." Like USAID and the
Peace Corps, its first concern is the proper placement and use
of the aid-giver, not the long term needs of the aid-receiver.

FROM THE VOLUNTEER'S
PERSPECTIVE

MANY PEACE CORPS volunteers would argue that their placement had little or nothing to do with the larger policy
objectives of the US government. One volunteer working in
the mountain region of the Philippines had no contact with the
Peace Corps office, USAID, or any other Peace Corps volunteer
in his two years of service. "I arrived at the community and
worked out my role with them," he explained. Most volunteers
believe that their service had a positive impact, independent of
the other agencies and policy initiatives of the US government.
"I worked with women to develop composting techniques and
planting vegetables," said a volunteer working in Honduras.
"These are techniques that will benefit them for a lifetime."

Despite the fact that some Peace Corps volunteers have
struggled to keep their work autonomous from US government
policy (in 1990, volunteers protested director Paul Coverdell's
move to rename the organization The United States Peace
Corps), the link is inherent. Federal lawmakers have referred
to the link as a matter of course. "If there is a person in the
Peace Corps who feels he cannot support US foreign policy,
then he ought not to be in the Peace Corps," stated Senator
Ross Adair (R-Ind). Loret Miller Ruppe, director of the Peace
Corps for eight years, proclaimed proudly at the outset of her
tenure that she hoped to prove her agency's work "a valuable
source of real aid to US foreign policy."

In general, expressions of dissent from federal doctrine
are strongly discouraged. During the Vietnam War, the Peace
Corps stipulated that no public disapproval of the war would

be tolerated, and in a widely publicized incident, a volunteer in Chile was dismissed after he wrote a letter denouncing the war to a Chilean newspaper. Yet even keeping one's views silent and working diligently to encourage real development may not be a sufficient shield from policy imperatives. A pair of volunteers in Honduras in the 1980s were commanded to "name the names" of local citizens that their sector boss believed were communists. Prospective volunteers should look closely at their placement and determine how their views may be inhibited by their affiliation.

Other criticisms have been leveled at the Peace Corps over the years. Former volunteers and staff have accused the agency of providing insufficient training, of defining goals and tasks too vaguely, of withholding follow-through, hindering the long term sustainability of projects. Returnees note that the Peace Corps often uses the presence or number of volunteers sent as a bargaining chip in its relations with other countries. During the 1980s, Central American ally nations were flooded with volunteers to counterbalance the heightened US military presence there and to put a good face on the intervention. "We were the Marines in velvet gloves," read a leaflet written and distributed by the radical Committee of Returned Volunteers in 1970.

Despite all the concerns about the Peace Corps as an arm of US foreign policy, the agency must be credited with enabling thousands of American citizens to witness the realities of poverty and injustice in the Third World. The refrain one hears over and over again in reviewing statements from returned volunteers is "I got much more than I gave." Most Peace Corps volunteers will attest that living and working alongside poor communities was the most powerful experience of their lives, one which has influenced their decisions and actions ever since.

Many returned Peace Corps volunteers have learned through their placement the intimate connections between development and economic justice, militarization and human rights. They return to the US and work to make US foreign and domestic policy more accountable to the poor.

As one returned Peace Corps volunteer explained, "If there is one thing to thank the Peace Corps for, it's for showing me how US policies hurt the average person. In a country like Paraguay, it is hard to miss the connection between US aid and the oppression of the poor. It is hard to miss the links between the IMF economic package and the inability of the poor to feed themselves. These realizations radically changed my perspectives on the world."

THE ROLE OF CIVIL SOCIETY

THE ORGANIZATIONS IN this book work in cooperation with NGOs and citizens' groups—not the government—in countries receiving volunteers. International cooperation among these groups is no guarantee against waste or misguided efforts, but at least the work that gets accomplished is much less likely to be confused with or compromised by the agendas of government, either ours or someone else's.

Much has been said and written over the last decade about the proliferation of nongovernmental organizations throughout the world and their potential for enacting social and political change. In countries of the developing and developed worlds—of the global South and the global North—the last ten years have witnessed a massive upsurge in the number of citizens' organizations airing grievances, lobbying for redress, mobilizing protests, establishing needed services for their constituents, and advocating for democratization of the forces of market and state. Concurrent has been the rise of resource or support organizations, often but not exclusively in the North, that provide research, advice, information, grants, or other aid to citizens' groups or to broader political aims. Both kinds of groups are referred to generally under the rubric of NGOs, or civil society, or the voluntary or third sector—as in a sector separate from both the market and the state. Lester Salamon, director of the Institute for Policy Studies at Johns Hopkins University, has used the term "associational revolution" to describe the growing size and strength of civil society groups. Their appeal to believers throughout the political spectrum is considerable, and their successes have inspired much optimism that they can accomplish what market and state have failed to bring about. To name just one example, concerted networking among hundreds of civil society organizations put thousands of protesters on the streets of Seattle during the WTO's Third Ministerial Conference in 1999.

Yet it is easy to overstate the importance of the third sector. In their book, *How to Live Your Dream of Volunteering Overseas,* Joseph Collins, Stefano DeZerega, and Zahara Heckscher sum up a few of the potential pitfalls of NGO-based volunteer endeavors:

> "The term NGO refers to tiny grassroots organizations with no staff as well as huge businesslike entities that get most of their funding from foreign governments. Smaller groups often have the greatest needs, but sometimes they find it hard to supervise volunteers effectively. Larger organizations may have more capacity to manage international volunteers, but can be more removed from the lives of local people. If a volunteer placement organization says that it works with local organizations, find out exactly what type of organizations they mean."

Civil society cannot by itself substitute for a failing economy or remove an authoritarian regime. A few of the points we have made against government interference and in favor of self help would fit comfortably into a conservative tract on the best way to aid the poor, and the more enthusiastic tributes to the third sector as a force for social good often neglect to consider the other two sectors as powers for both good and bad. The emphasis on third sector solutions can conceal a retreat from necessary government-supported solutions to poverty and injustice, such as agrarian reform or income redistribution. In the present day, when fifty-one of the hundred largest

economies in the world are transnational corporations, one cannot be too sanguine about the strength of the market or the role
governments play in enforcing inequalities of wealth. The presence of civil society in and of itself is not a cure for social
problems. It is a powerful tool, but one tool among several.

Nevertheless, the future of nongovernmental organizations
appears promising. These days USAID and the Peace Corps
employ the rhetoric of "grassroots empowerment" and "local
decision-making" in describing their own projects. We welcome
this sign of the trickling-up of NGO influence, and can only
hope that there is sufficient substance behind the words to make
a real difference in some people's lives. Meanwhile, readers of
this guide are encouraged to involve themselves in truly sustainable development, and to consider programs not necessarily
averse to government endorsement, but having no need of it.

OPTIONS FOR VOLUNTEERING

ONCE YOU HAVE clarified your personal objectives, it's time to consider what type of placement makes the most sense for you. Listed in the resource guide are a number of established agencies and programs that offer service opportunities in a wide range of countries and settings. You may also consider one of the following alternatives which may be more appropriate for your particular interests.

Designing Your Own Experience

Some of the most exciting possibilities for working abroad can be designed independently according to your interests and beliefs. One option is to identify an organization and communicate directly about working as a volunteer. By researching grassroots organizations, you will learn more about their needs and the types of skills they can use. Remember, the longer you stay in community, the greater the difference you can make.

You can begin by reviewing alternative publications, development journals, and the annual reports of organizations that fund projects such as Oxfam, Grassroots International, International Development Exchange (IDEX), or the Global Fund for Women. We have listed several websites under Other Organizations that link to, list, or discuss grassroots groups throughout the world.

Keep in mind that it is a mistake to assume that all grassroots organizations need or want volunteers. Some groups are suspicious of the idea of unpaid labor in any context, and prefer to retain only a tiny but paid staff. Some emphasize the values of mutual aid and local empowerment to the point of not wanting volunteers from outside the community served. Do not presume that, with a little coaxing or bargaining, you can overcome the resistance of someone who says no to your offer to volunteer. When you contact organizations, clearly state your goals, expectations, skills, and length of time you are available. The organization can then decide if you can be of service in its work.

Learning as a Student

Another option is to go overseas as a student. A number of universities offer study abroad programs that provide an opportunity to learn about the political, economic, and social conditions in a given country. Once established in a country, you can seek out individuals and groups directly involved with community development. They may be able to direct you to an appropriate volunteer placement where you can build your skills and experience in the field.

Short Term Opportunities

A long term commitment may not be necessary. If your goal is to gain a better understanding of the world and learn from the experiences of others, you can choose one or several short term trips or work exchange programs. There are a number of groups like Global Exchange that conduct exposure tours in the Third World. These are socially responsible educational tours that provide participants unmediated experience of the political, economic, and social structures that create or promote hunger, poverty, and environmental degradation. Tours offer an opportunity to meet people with diverse perspectives on agriculture, development, and the environment. They often include the opportunity to stay with local people, visit rural areas, and meet with grassroots organizers. Such tours can alter your understanding of hunger and poverty and direct you to areas where you can best work for democratic social change.

Whether you decide on an organized volunteer program, a tour, or to go on your own, it is essential to do your homework beforehand. Read as much as possible about the country (especially its history and politics), learn about groups working in the area, write in advance to groups that interest you, and talk to people at home who know about the area you are considering.

COMMON QUESTIONS

How can I finance my stay if I don't go through an established program?

While some agencies offer a stipend, insurance, and travel, many smaller programs are not able to offer these benefits. For many people, financing is the greatest obstacle. It is often the primary reason for going through a government or church organization. (Agencies run by religious congregations can generally afford to be far more generous than the non-sectarian ones.) Many volunteers are attracted by the option to defer student loans during the period of their placement; student loans can be deferred while participating full time in any tax exempt volunteer agency. In responding to our requests for updated information, a few of the organizations here mentioned that their volunteers are eligible for AmeriCorps grants upon completion of service. Some indicated that they provide fundraising advice or assistance. It might be worthwhile to inquire if the organization you apply to offers similar arrangements.

There are alternative funding sources to consider for overseas work. Scholarships, fellowships, or loans are also available. You may find funds to pay travel expenses by going through a university or language study program. Some university departments have research funds that are available to both undergraduate and graduate students. A public library, career service center, or specialized library like the Foundation Center—with branches throughout the country—are sources for information on grants and loans. Many untapped resources may be found in local governments, private associations, and

church groups. For example, the Rotary Club offers scholarships for foreign travel, and many churches support their
parishioners in return for educational service upon return
from an overseas trip.

Friends and relatives are another possible source of funds.
You may be able to arrange a personal loan or an exchange.
One woman who traveled throughout Central America for a
year started her own newsletter and asked friends and family
to subscribe to help subsidize her living expenses.

The first source may be your own bank account. Look at
the possibility of working to save money for a trip. Airfare will
be your primary expense; living in the Third World, especially
in rural areas, is by and large extremely affordable. If you can
arrange an internship or a work exchange (like teaching
English) for room and board, your living expenses can be
kept to a minimum.

Do I need technical skills?

Generally, the demand for unskilled volunteers is low. While
some groups offer opportunities for "generalists," other
organizations with long term commitments to development
in a given area may require specialized skills not available
locally. In considering volunteer opportunities, it's important
to ask if you would be taking a job that could be done by a local
person. If you are offering a new skill to an area, you should
investigate whether the program involves transferring that skill
to local people.

In any work experience, local people can best define your
role. Let them know what your skills are and allow them to
decide how they can best put those skills to use. A volunteer

who went to work with a community organization in
Mexico learned that his most useful skill was puppet-making.
He didn't know before he arrived that street theater is a popu-
lar form of political communication. When a local clinic
learned that he was an artist and an actor, they suggested that
he help them communicate health care information through
puppet shows. There are many organizations that take volunteers with specific technical skills, such as construction, health
care, and agriculture.

Do I have to be Christian to be a volunteer with one of the church agencies?

Listed in the resource guide are some volunteer programs with
religious affiliations. We have tried to select programs that hold
as their primary purpose the support of local efforts at community development, and to steer clear of any that are evangelical.
Some do require a commitment to a certain faith, but most ask
only that the volunteer share a concern for social justice. As
with any volunteer placement, it is important to understand the
values behind an agency's volunteer program clearly.

What are the possibilities for getting paid work overseas?

Most overseas development positions require two or more
years of community development experience. While a two-year
volunteer post does not guarantee future employment, you may
find that by developing your skills and connections with Third
World communities, job possibilities will open up. To guide

you in your job search, you will find organizations and
publications in the Resources section which list employment
openings overseas.

EVALUATING
AN ORGANIZATION

NO MATTER WHICH voluntary service organization you are considering, get answers to these questions before making a commitment:

What is the political or religious affiliation of the organization? Is the purpose of the organization to convert or influence poor people to adopt new cultural, economic, or social values?

Who funds the organization? Do the funding sources have political or religious affiliations that may influence the organization's programs?

Is the organization working with local or national governments? Overtly or covertly? Under the auspices of another institution?

In what countries does the organization have programs? In what countries does it NOT have programs, and why?

These questions are hard to answer with the information supplied in brochures or publicity materials. Look beyond the brochures. Get a list of program alumni and ask them about their experiences, write to people in the field, find out who is critical of the program and why. The section, Food First Books of Related Interest, lists several books that take a critical look at development organizations overseas.

BRINGING THE
LESSONS HOME

LIVING ABROAD AND working with poor communities to confront the causes of hunger and poverty can have a long-lasting
impact on your life. It can deepen your understanding of the
tremendous power the US has over the lives of people around
the world: to make and break governments; to affect the world
economy through trade, investment, and foreign aid policies;
and to influence economic priorities through USAID, the World
Bank, the International Monetary Fund, and the World Trade
Organization.

Going abroad will be educational, but that is only the beginning. Experience with a disenfranchised community means
taking the responsibility of bringing your experiences home.
The lessons learned may have direct applications: working to
end hunger and poverty in our own country, pressuring the US
government to end its involvement with repressive regimes,
limiting arms sales to the Third World, and holding US corporations accountable for their actions overseas. Several of the
organizations listed here expect volunteers to carry out educational work on their return home, and will provide you with
advice on how it might best be done.

There are many ways in which a Third World experience
can be translated into work at home. A Peace Corps volunteer
who served with Guatemalan Indians returned to the US and
worked with Native Americans in Arizona. A health care
volunteer with an international organization in Ghana found
work at a free clinic in California. An agricultural extension
worker who volunteered in Mozambique became active in the

movement to stop US support of South Africa's apartheid regime. These examples and others show that experience in a marginalized community is often the catalyst for taking action in our own country to create more democratic organizations and policies at the local, national, and international levels, and to help ensure the survival of grassroots efforts all over the world.

A WORD ON THE LISTINGS

IN COMPILING THE following list of organizations we looked
for groups that address the political and economic causes of
poverty. In our view, these programs place volunteers in positions that complement the work of local people, grassroots
organizations, and nongovernmental organizations (NGOs).
Many on the list are not traditional voluntary service organizations. They may have programs that send volunteers abroad, but
their main purpose is educational work in the US. Through
service and work projects, their aim is to build lasting links
between communities at home and abroad.

A few of our evident discriminations may seem a bit arbi-
trary. A command of the English language has without question
become a desirable attainment in many developing nations, but
we've listed none of the organizations that deal strictly in sending English teachers overseas. We have included only a few of
the organizations devoted to sending teachers abroad on the
grounds that most of those programs serve primarily the host
countries' middle or professional classes. We have added an
organization that connects volunteers to organic farms internationally, despite the fact that the program does not work
directly with the poor. Our view is that the development of
alternative systems of agriculture is in itself a vital contribution
to a more equitable and sustainable distribution of resources.

The listings are by no means comprehensive. Many organizations are so small and take so few volunteers that they prefer
not to be listed. Hundreds of other possibilities are not mentioned because they are not formal volunteer programs. Every
community, school, church, and labor union has the potential
for developing international programs that send delegates

abroad, initiate ongoing partnership programs, and offer direct assistance to Third World communities. These opportunities are often the most exciting, but must be created by the volunteer.

Alternatives to the Peace Corps provides a starting point to explore the options for volunteering. Through your own research of these organizations and others, you can choose the appropriate options available to you. For more information, see the Other Organizations section in the back of this book. *Alternatives to the Peace Corps* is an ongoing project of Food First. This guide will be updated again in the future. We rely on the comments and recommendations of our readers to improve each new edition. We welcome your suggestions for changes or additions.

Please note that most of the organizations listed in the resource guide function on very small budgets. If you are writing to request information, please enclose a self-addressed stamped envelope.

References

Chao, Elaine L. "Today's Peace Corps," address to National Press Club, Washington, DC, May 5, 1992.

Chasin, Barbara H. and Richard W. Franke. *Kerala: Radical Reform as Development in an Indian State* (Oakland, CA: Food First Books, 1994).

Chinn, Erica and Kristina Taylor, eds. *The Pros and Cons of the Peace Corps*. JustAct: Youth Action for Global Justice, 333 Valencia Street, Suite 101, San Francisco, California 94103.

CIVICUS. *Civil Society at the Millennium* (West Hartford, CT: Kumarian Press, 1999).

Collins, Joseph, Stefano DeZerega, and Zahara Heckscher. *How to Live Your Dream of Volunteering Overseas* (New York: Viking Penguin, 2001)

Collins, Joseph, Frances Moore Lappé and Peter Rosset with Luis Esparza. *World Hunger: Twelve Myths* (New York: Grove Press, 1998).

Fischer, Fritz. *Making Them Like Us: Peace Corps Volunteers in the 1960s* (Washington, DC: Smithsonian Institution Press, 1998).

Kutzner, Patricia L. and Nicola Lagoudakis, with Teresa Eyring. *Who's Involved with Hunger: An Organization Guide for Education and Advocacy* (Washington, DC: World Hunger Education Service, 1995).

Lappé, Frances Moore and Rachel Schurman. *Taking Population Seriously* (Oakland, CA: Food First Books, 1990).

MacMartin, Charley. "Peace Corps and Empire," *Covert Action Quarterly*, Winter 1991–1992, no. 39.

McAllister, Bill. "Peace Corps Plans to Send 500 to Ex-Soviet States," *The Washington Post*, December 31, 1991, pg. A11.

Razzi, Elizabeth. "What the Peace Corps Can Do for You," *Kiplinger's Personal Finance Magazine*, June 1998.

Reeves, T. Zane. *The Politics of the Peace Corps and VISTA* (Tuscaloosa, AL: University of Alabama Press, 1988).

Schwarz, Karen. *What You Can Do For Your Country: Inside the Peace Corps—A Thirty-Year History* (New York: William Morrow, 1993).

Watson, Bruce. "The New Peace Corps Steppes Out—in Kazakhstan," *Smithsonian*, August 1994, vol. 25 no. 5.

Zimmerman, Jonathan. "Beyond Double Consciousness: Black Peace Corps Volunteers in Africa, 1961–1971," *Journal of American History*, December 1995, vol. 82, no. 3.

Personal interview with returned Peace Corps volunteer who asked to remain anonymous.

Websites of AmeriCorps (www.americorps.org), Catholic Worker (www.catholicworker.org), CIVICUS (www.civicus.org), InterAction (www.interaction.org), Peace Corps (www.peacecorps.gov), VISTA (www.friendsofvista.org), and USAID (www.usaid.gov).

INTERNATIONAL VOLUNTARY
SERVICE ORGANIZATIONS

THE FOLLOWING ORGANIZATIONS offer opportunities to
work with impoverished people in the Third World. These
voluntary service organizations are selected for their common
approach to combating poverty, emphasizing support of grassroots efforts to empower poor people.

Abya Yala Fund

678 13th Street, Suite 100, Oakland, CA 94612
Tel: (510) 763-6553   Fax: (510) 763-6588
E-mail: abyayala@earthlink.net   Website: ayf.nativeweb.org
🍂 Abya Yala is an organization providing resources and technical
training to indigenous people from South and Central America
and Mexico. The group works to help indigenous peoples
address development issues in their communities, in a culturally
appropriate and environmentally sustainable way. Plans for
opening regional offices in Central and South America will open
opportunities for overseas volunteer work by 2001. Preferably,
interns should speak Spanish.

Adventures in Health, Education, and Agricultural Development, Inc. (AHEAD, Inc.)

PO Box 2049, Rockville, MD 20847-2049
Tel: (301) 530-3697   Fax: (301) 530-3532
E-mail: info@aheadinc.org   Website: www.aheadinc.org
🍂 AHEAD (Adventures in Health, Education, and Agricultural
Development) combats malnutrition, disease, and poverty
through people-to-people exchanges and support of grassroots
initiatives. Since 1985, AHEAD has provided opportunities for

professionals as well as graduate and undergraduate students to
work as volunteers side-by-side with their African counterparts
in community projects in rural Tanzania and the Gambia.
AHEAD's programs emphasize child survival and safe mother-
hood, focusing on teen pregnancy prevention, HIV/AIDS and
STD prevention, immunizations, nutrition, family planning,
women's health, and youth leadership development.

The Summer Volunteer Program for undergraduates runs
six to eight weeks and cost of participation is $4000, airfare
included. Length and cost of programs for graduates and professionals vary; contact AHEAD for details. Volunteers are
encouraged to fundraise for their trips. All contributions to
AHEAD, Inc. are tax-deductible.

American Friends Service Committee

1501 Cherry Street, Philadelphia, PA 19102-1479

Tel: (215) 241-7295   Fax: (215) 241-7247

E-mail: mexsummer@afsc.org   Website: www.afsc.org

✎ American Friends Service Committee (AFSC) sponsors
summer programs in Mexico for people ages 18 to 26. The
community service program in Mexico runs from early June
to the end of July. Participants live in rural villages. They work
under the direction of Mexican organizations and respond to
the needs of the particular community in which they live.
Applicants should have skills in construction, gardening,
arts, crafts, child care, or other practical areas. Proficiency in
Spanish is necessary. Prior experience in community service
and organizing is very helpful. Participants pay a $950 fee for
seven weeks and cover their own travel expenses. A limited
number of scholarships are available, as are several paid
facilitator positions.

Amigos de las Americas

5618 Star Lane, Houston, TX 77057

Tel: (800) 231-7796   Fax: (713) 782-9267

E-mail: info@amigoslink.org   Website: www.amigoslink.org

🌢 Amigos de las Americas accepts volunteers 16 years or
older to work in teams in Latin America. They provide health
services at schools, health clinics, and in communities. In
addition to bringing technical knowledge and supplies to the
project, volunteers assume leadership roles as health educators.
Amigos chapters and training groups across the US conduct
training prior to departure and raise funds for the majority
of volunteers. The cost is approximately $3000, but may
vary depending on the area of placement. The fee covers all
expenses, including housing with a family. At least one year
of Spanish is a prerequisite. There are currently programs in
Mexico, Costa Rica, the Dominican Republic, Nicaragua,
Paraguay, Brazil, Honduras, and Bolivia.

Amizade, Ltd.

367 South Graham Street, Pittsburgh, PA 15232

Tel: (888) 973-4443   Fax: (412) 648-1492

E-mail: Volunteer@amizade.org   Website: www.amizade.org

🌢 Amizade is a nonprofit organization dedicated to promoting
volunteerism and providing community service in locations
throughout the world. Amizade programs offer a mix of community service and recreation, providing volunteers with the
opportunity to participate firsthand in the culture of the region
to which they travel. Past projects have included constructing
a vocational training center for street children in the Amazon
region, building additional rooms on a health clinic in the
Bolivian Andes, and performing historical preservation and
environmental cleanup in the Yellowstone area. Volunteers do

not need any special skills, just a willingness to help. Amizade
has programs in Brazil, Bolivia, Australia, and Navajo Nation
and Greater Yellowstone Region, USA. No scholarships are
available.

International programs (Brazil, Bolivia, Australia) run two to
four weeks and cost $1500 per two weeks; domestic programs
run one to two weeks and cost $600 per week. Fees include
room, board, and recreational activities.

Bikes Not Bombs

59 Amory Street, Apartment 103, Roxbury, MA 02119
Tel: (617) 442-0004   Fax: (617) 445-2439
E-mail: bnbrox@igc.org   Website: www.bikesnotbombs.org

🚲 Bikes Not Bombs (BNB) is a nonprofit grassroots development and solidarity organization that helps local groups form
ecologically viable bicycle workshops and related projects in
Central America, the Caribbean, and the US. These projects
have involved the collecting of over 17,000 donated bicycles
and tons of parts from across the US, recycling them to
Nicaragua, Haiti, the Dominican Republic, and recently to
Bikes Not Bombs' own inner city youth programs in Boston.
BNB provides technical assistance, training, tools, and financing
for these projects and funds a bicycle-purchaser-revolving loan
fund for campesinos in Nicaragua. Experienced bilingual
mechanics and personnel are placed to carry out field work.
Send a resume and cover letter.

Brethren Volunteer Services

1451 Dundee Avenue, Elgin, IL 60120
Tel: (847) 742-5100 or (800) 323-8039   Fax: (847) 742-6103
E-mail: bvs_gb@brethren.org   Website: www.brethren.org

🍂 Brethren Volunteer Services is a program grounded in Christian faith that brings a spiritual dimension to advocating justice, working for peace, serving basic human needs, and maintaining the integrity of creation. Brethren Volunteer Services (BVS) places volunteers in Latin America, Europe, and Africa. BVS also has one year programs in the US. Positions abroad last two years and begin with a three-week orientation in the US. Volunteers are involved in a variety of community services: education, health care, office/secretarial work, and construction work. Volunteers can also participate in ministry to children, youth, senior citizens, homeless, victims of domestic violence, prisoners, refugees, and persons with AIDS. Some positions require knowledge of a foreign language prior to orientation. Other requirements and special skills vary with assignments. Volunteers need not be Brethren or Christian, but should have an interest in examining the Christian faith. A college degree or equivalent life experience is required for overseas assignments. Travel expenses, room and board, medical coverage, and a monthly stipend of about $50 are provided.

Child Family Health International

2149 Lyon Street, #5, San Francisco, CA 94115
Tel: (415) 863-4900   Fax: (501) 432-6852
E-mail: cfhi@cfhi.org   Website: www.cfhi.org

🍂 Child Family Health International (CFHI) is a nonprofit organization providing health services to poor communities worldwide by supporting local projects with essential medical supplies, volunteers, and funding. CFHI sends US medical, pre-medical, and public health students to Ecuador, Mexico, and India for training and service-learning. Duties include hospital or clinical rotations and community education and outreach.

Participants should view their CFHI clerkships as opportunities to develop cross-cultural and community health awareness, rather than to provide humanitarian aid. Programs vary in length from three to twelve weeks. Spanish proficiency or near-proficiency is required for most of the placements in Ecuador and Mexico. CFHI accepts allied health professionals and non-medical students to certain of its programs; refer to the website for more details.

Christian Peacemaker Teams

PO Box 6508, Chicago, IL 60680-6508

Tel: (312) 455-1199   Fax: (312) 432-1213
E-mail: cpt@igc.org   Website: www.prairienet.org/cpt

🌶 Christian Peacemaker Teams (CPT) is a project of the Quakers, Mennonites, and Church of the Brethren. CPT leads short term study delegations several times yearly to areas of conflict and/or heightened militarization and organizes longer-term volunteers—the Christian Peacemaker Corps—to perform protective witness and accompaniment work in the West Bank, Chiapas, Vieques, Colombia, and Native American communities in the US and Canada. Teams of two to twelve persons join the efforts of local peacemakers facing imminent violence. They accompany threatened individuals, report on human rights abuses, plan and execute nonviolent public responses to injustice, and train others in nonviolent direct action.

CPT emphasizes the Christian nature of its commitment to peace. All Corps volunteers must attend training in nonviolent direct action, either at CPT headquarters in Chicago or at regional sessions offered if demand is sufficient. Candidates pay their own way to training; if accepted, full-time Corps members receive a small monthly stipend based on their living expenses, and are expected to seek contributions to CPT in support of their work. CPT also maintains a reserve Corps of trained volunteers on-call for short periods of time. Corps volunteers and reservists must be 21 or older. Study tour participants are self-funded and should be at least 18 years of age.

Committee for Health Rights in the Americas (CHRIA)
474 Valencia Street, Suite 120, San Francisco, CA 94103
Tel: (415) 431-7760   Fax: (415) 431-7768
E-mail: chria@igc.org   Website: www.chria.org
⟡ The Committee for Health Rights in the Americas (CHRIA) promotes universal health rights across borders through grassroots organizing, advocacy, public education, coalition building, international educational exchanges, and medical and technical assistance. CHRIA's volunteer program, the Training Exchange, places licensed health care workers fluent in Spanish in long term (minimum six months) assignments in Central America. Assignments focus on providing training to health professionals, health promoters, and other health workers. Volunteers receive travel assistance and a modest stipend.

Concern America
2015 North Broadway, Santa Ana, CA 92706
Mailing address: PO Box 1790, Santa Ana, CA 92702
Tel: (714) 953-8575 or (800) CON-CERN   Fax: (714) 953-1242
E-mail: concamerinc@earthlink.net
Website: www.concernamerica.org
⟡ Concern America is an international development and refugee aid organization whose main objective is to provide training, technical assistance, and material support to community-based programs in Third World countries and

refugee camps. Concern America volunteers serve for at least two years, and are professionals such as physicians, nurses, nutritionists, community organizers, and specialists in agriculture, appropriate technology, public health, and sanitation. The focus of the work is on training local people to carry on programs that include health care training, developing nutrition and sanitation projects, organizing community development and income-generating projects, and conducting literacy campaigns. Concern America volunteers currently serve in El Salvador, Honduras, Guatemala, Mexico, and Mozambique. Volunteers must be at least 21 and fluent in Spanish. Concern America provides transportation, room and board, health insurance, and a small stipend. In addition, a repatriation allowance of $50 per month of service is provided to the volunteer upon completion of contract.

Cristianos por la Paz en El Salvador (CRISPAZ)

319 Camden, San Antonio, TX 78215

Tel: (210) 222-2018   Fax: (210) 226-9119

E-mail: crispaz@igc.org   Website: www.crispaz.org

🐱 Founded in 1984, CRISPAZ, or Christians for Peace in El Salvador, is a faith-based organization dedicated to mutual accompaniment with the church of the poor and marginalized communities in El Salvador. In building bridges of solidarity between communities in El Salvador and those in their home countries, CRISPAZ volunteers strive together for peace, justice, and human liberation. The long term volunteer program is designed for individuals who wish to spend a minimum of one year living and working in a marginalized urban or rural community in El Salvador. Long term volunteers give of their time, skills, and interests as they work alongside Salvadorans in areas such as literacy, health care, pastoral work, community organization, education, agriculture, appropriate technology, and youth work.

The summer immersion program is designed to provide an intensive learning and service experience in a poor community in El Salvador. Interns live with Salvadorans and accompany them in their daily lives and work. Each intern will have the opportunity to contribute his or her skills to the communities. CRISPAZ provides volunteers with orientation, project placement, and support throughout the term of service. El Salvador Encounter is a faith-based experience in which participants can learn about current Salvadoran reality. Encounters are seven to ten days long and offer the opportunity to explore a different reality and build relationships with people of a different culture.

Cross-Cultural Solutions

47 Potter Avenue, New Rochelle, NY 10801
Tel. (800) 380-4777 or (914) 632-0022   Fax: (914) 632-8494
E-mail: info@crossculturalsolutions.org
Website: www.crossculturalsolutions.org

♪ Cross-Cultural Solutions offers exciting volunteer programs in India, Ghana, China, Cuba, and Peru. These programs provide short term opportunities to volunteers who desire to contribute to vital global issues while experiencing the rich cultures of these countries. If you have three weeks or more and an open mind, you can volunteer in India, Ghana, China, Cuba, or Peru and work with outstanding local service organizations for positive change. No prior volunteer experience is necessary. All backgrounds and levels of experience are welcome.

Cross-Cultural Solutions will handle all the details related to your volunteer program. Volunteer positions fall into three main categories: health care, education, and community development. The cost for the three-week experience is $1950. This includes orientation, training materials, coordination, professional staff, lodging, transportation, transfers, and meals. Your fee does not include international airfare, insurance, visa fees, or spending money. All expenses are tax-deductible. Your entire program fee goes directly to expenses related to your volunteer program. Cross-Cultural Solutions can also provide a fundraising kit to help volunteers raise money for their expenses.

Doctors Without Borders USA, Inc.
Médecins Sans Frontières USA, Inc.
In New York:

6 East 39th Street, 8th Floor, New York, NY 10016

Tel: (212) 679-6800 or (888) 392-0392   Fax: (212) 679-7016

E-mail: dwb@newyork.msf.org   Website: www.dwb.org

In Los Angeles:

2040 Avenue of the Stars, C-216, Los Angeles, CA 90067

Tel: (310) 277-2793   Fax: (310) 277-1667

E-mail: msf-losangeles@msf.org

🔥 Doctors Without Borders (known internationally as Médecins Sans Frontières, or MSF) is the world's largest independent emergency medical relief organization. Each year over 2000 doctors, nurses, other medical professionals, and logistical experts from 45 nations volunteer to work in more than 80 countries around the world. They assist victims of war, civil strife, epidemics, and natural disasters, without discrimination of race, religion, creed, or political affiliation.

Solid professional experience is essential in the field. All medical professionals must have a valid license to practice and must have had two years of post-graduate professional work experience. The minimum volunteer commitment is six

months; a year's commitment is more typical. A good working
knowledge of a foreign language is highly valued. Familiarity
with tropical medicine is an asset. For more information and/or
an application form, please call or visit the website.

The Fellows Program

c/o JustAct—Youth Action for Global Justice
333 Valencia Street, Suite 101, San Francisco, CA 94103-3547
Tel: (415) 431-4480   Fax: (415) 431-5953
E-mail: fellowship@lafetra.org   Website: www.lafetra.org

The Fellows Program offers a unique international fellowship
combining volunteer work abroad with service learning in the
Bay Area. Fellows experience cross-cultural exchange firsthand
and receive a stipend, a travel grant, and training to support
their work with local and international organizations. The program runs for nine months in three stages: first an internship at
a Bay Area community-based organization, then a two- to three-
month volunteer project abroad, followed by a return to the
Bay Area internship where Fellows focus on ways to apply their
overseas experience at home and in future work. Pre-service
and re-entry retreats and periodic workshops are also included
in the fellowship.

The program is committed to making international service
a viable option for people of color and individuals from low
income backgrounds, in recognition of the fact that even the
most outstanding international volunteer programs have low
rates of participation among such persons. Candidates must be
at least 18 years of age, US citizens or residents, with demon-
strated financial need, who have worked for positive change in
their communities, had limited opportunity to travel abroad,
and no previous international volunteer experience.
Applications are due in December for fellowships that begin

in March of the following year. Contact Viviana Rennella at the
above address for further information.

Foundation for Sustainable Development

5547 Mitcham Court, Springfield, VA 22151
Tel: (703) 764-0859
E-mail: fsd@unc.edu
Website: www.fsd-latinamerica.com

📝 The Foundation for Sustainable Development is a private,
nonprofit organization dedicated to providing economic
alternatives to college students and graduates who want hands-
on community development experience in Africa and Latin
America. The two-month summer internship program includes
an internship with a grassroots development organization, a
family homestay, and orientation and evaluation sessions.
Internship areas include community development, environmental preservation, women's issues, health, education, nutrition,
youth development, and sustainable agriculture. Individual
internships are also available throughout the year for all lengths
of time. Programs are located primarily in Nicaragua and
Bolivia. Program costs vary. Credit and scholarships may be
available. Knowledge of Spanish and a 3.0 GPA are required.
Please see the web page for more information about programs,
prerequisites, costs and/or to print out an application.

Fourth World Movement

7600 Willow Hill Drive, Landover, MD 20785-4658
Tel: (301) 336-9489   Fax: (301) 336-0092
E-mail: fourthworld@erols.com
Website: www.atd-fourthworld.org

📝 Fourth World Movement's work is based on three priorities:
learning from the most disadvantaged families, understanding

how they become trapped in persistent poverty, and planning and developing projects with them. Volunteers must first participate in a two- to three-month internship, living and working with full time volunteers at the New York and Washington, DC area centers. Interns learn about the Movement and its approach to persistent poverty through their work, and through videos, readings, and discussion. At the end of the internship, interns discuss with their supervisor what their two year assignment will be. Placement is made according to both the interns' interests and the Movement's needs. There are currently teams in 24 countries. Participants contribute toward food costs during the internship and receive a small stipend during their assignment.

Summer work camps are also available at the international center in France. Work camp volunteers are age 18 and older and participate in a fourteen-day program where they learn about poverty and do various kinds of manual work.

Frontier Internship in Mission

International Coordinating Office
Ecumenical Center
150 Route de Ferney, 1211 Geneva 2, SWITZERLAND
Tel: 41 (22) 798-8987   Fax: 41 (22) 788-1434
E-mail: jm@tfim.org   Website: www.tfim.org

🍂 Frontier Internship in Mission (FIM) is an international ecumenical internship program that provides people between 20 and 35 years of age with the opportunity to work abroad on social issues for two years. The program emphasizes new forms of ecumenical mission in the context of justice, peace, and the ecosphere. FIM supports community-building, especially among poor people's organizations in Asia, Africa, and Latin America. Individuals applying to FIM should be a member of a

community engaged in justice concerns. Communities interested in receiving an intern propose a project to FIM;
communities wanting to send an intern to another region may
also apply. FIM Coordinating Office funds travel, subsistence
living allowance, and a one-year re-entry project with their
sending group after the two-year period overseas.

Frontiers Foundation/Operation Beaver
2615 Danforth Ave., Ste. 203, Toronto, Ontario, CANADA M4C 1L6
Tel: (416) 690-3930   Fax: (416) 690-3934
E-mail: frontiersfoundation@on.aibn.com
Website: www.frontiersfoundation.org
♪ Frontiers Foundation is a community development service
organization that works in partnership with communities in low
income rural areas across northern Canada. These locally initiated projects build and improve housing, conduct training
programs, and organize educational and recreational activities
in developing regions. Volunteers must be 18 or older and
available for a minimum of 12 weeks. Skills in carpentry,
electrical work, and plumbing are preferred for construction
projects. Previous social service and experience with
children are preferred for recreation and educational
projects. Accommodation, food, and travel inside Canada
are provided.

Global Citizens Network
(See listing under Alternative Travel and Study Overseas)

Global Routes
1814 Seventh Street, Suite A, Berkeley, CA 94710
Tel: (510) 848-4800   Fax: (510) 848-4801
E-mail: mail@globalroutes.org   Website: www.globalroutes.org

꒳ Global Routes, a nonprofit nongovernmental organization, sponsors community service and cultural exchange programs for North American high school and college students. Participants work side-by-side with their host families on projects selected by the community. These have included constructing schools, clinics, and community centers, and teaching and reforesting. High school programs exist in Kenya, Zimbabwe, St. Lucia, Bolivia, Ghana, Thailand, Vietnam, Nepal, Costa Rica, Ecuador, Belize, and Guadeloupe; college programs exist in Kenya, Ecuador, Costa Rica, Thailand, India, and the Navajo Reservation. Term-time sessions (fall, spring, and winter) are approximately three months long, summer sessions about two months. All expenses are paid by the participant.

Global Service Corps

Earth Island Institute

300 Broadway, Suite 28, San Francisco, CA 94133

Tel: (415) 788-3666, ext. 128   Fax: (415) 788-7324

E-mail: gsc@earthisland.org

Website: www.globalservicecorps.org

꒳ Global Service Corps, a project of Earth Island Institute, invites volunteers to join one of its short or long term programs in Costa Rica, Thailand, or Kenya. Assignments include sustainable agriculture and national park maintenance (Costa Rica), English teaching and health clinic assistance (Thailand), and HIV/AIDS education and biointensive gardening (Kenya). Short term placements run two to four weeks and can serve as orientation for long term ventures; long term programs run two months or longer, not including short term program time. Participants must be at least 20 years old. Specific skills—for example, in the fields of medicine or environmental science—are useful but not necessary. Volunteers pay all expenses.

Program fees paid in advance cover room, board, transportation within the assigned country, project materials, and entrance fees.

Global Volunteers

375 East Little Canada Road, St. Paul, MN 55117-1627
Tel: (800) 487-1074 or (651) 407-6100 Fax: (651) 482-0915
E-mail: email@globalvolunteers.org
Website: www.globalvolunteers.org

🌶 Global Volunteers forms teams of volunteers who live in host communities and work with local people on development projects selected by local leadership. The projects may involve construction and renovation of schools and clinics, health care, tutoring, business planning, or assisting in other local activities. Opportunities are available in Africa, Asia, the Caribbean, Europe, Latin America, and the Pacific Islands. Volunteers are of all ages and come from all backgrounds and occupations, including teachers, carpenters, homemakers, physicians, and artists. No special skills or languages are required. Tax-deductible program fees range from $450 to $2395 and include costs of training, ground transportation, lodging, project materials, all meals, and an experienced team leader.

Habitat for Humanity International

121 Habitat Street, Americus, GA 31709
Tel: (229) 924-6935 or (800) 422-4828 Fax: (229) 924-0641
E-mail: public_info@habitat.org Website: www.habitat.org

🌶 Habitat for Humanity International (HFHI) is an ecumenical Christian housing ministry whose goal is to eliminate substandard housing from the world. Habitat's philosophy is to empower people to establish a sustainable grassroots housing program in their own communities.

International Partners is a part of HFHI. International Partners volunteers serve at international assignments for a minimum of three years in the areas of affiliate development and national program development. Much of the work involves training/teaching, leadership and community development, and mentoring of the local and national boards in all aspects of the Habitat programs. IPs receive a monthly living allowance, housing, insurance, travel expenses, and a re-entry bonus. Candidates must complete a training course held twice a year in the spring and fall. They should be 21 or older and willing to communicate HFHI's Christian roots and principles.

Construction and office-related work is also available in Habitat's affiliates in the US and in the International Headquarters in Americus, Georgia. Volunteers at the head-quarters must be 18 years or older. They receive training, free housing, and a small weekly stipend.

IFCO/Pastors for Peace

402 West 145th Street, New York, NY 10031

Tel: (212) 926-5757   Fax: (212) 926-5842

E-mail: ifco@igc.org   Website: www.ifconews.org

🌿 Pastors for Peace is an action/education project of the Interreligious Foundation for Community Organization (IFCO) and includes activists from all sectors of society. Anyone who works for peace with justice is a "pastor" for peace. Pastors for Peace organizes humanitarian aid caravans, work brigades, delegations, and study tours to Mexico, Central America, and Cuba. Churches, schools, and other organizations can name the dates and help define the itinerary of customized study tours and construction brigades for their members. Cost ranges from $550 to $1,150 depending on the project. Call Pastors for Peace for more information and applications.

Institute for International Cooperation and Development
PO Box 520, Williamstown, MA 01267

Tel: (413) 458-9828   Fax: (413) 458-3323

E-mail: iicd@berkshire.net   Website: www.iicd-volunteer.org

➴ The Institute for International Cooperation and Development (IICD) organizes travel, study, and solidarity courses in Africa, Latin America, and the US. The program is open to anyone 18 years and older. The IICD sends volunteer teams to Angola, Brazil, El Salvador, Guatemala, Honduras, India, Mozambique, Nicaragua, Zambia, and Zimbabwe. Volunteer projects include community health and AIDS prevention education, literacy and vocational skills teaching, school and clinic construction, agricultural extension with small-scale farmers, and teacher training.

Most programs are six to nineteen months, including preparation and follow-up periods in the US. Preparation entails language and practical training, regional studies, and fundraising. The follow-up period includes giving presentations and making educational materials about the visited regions. The cost varies depending on the program. Fee covers training, room, board, international insurance, and airfare. Fundraising ideas as well as some financial aid are available.

The International Partnership for Service-Learning
815 Second Avenue, Suite 315, New York, NY 10017-4594

Tel: (212) 986-0989   Fax: (212) 986-5039

E-mail: pslny@aol.com   Website: www.ipsl.com

➴ The Partnership's programs combine formal learning with extensive community service to those in need. The Partnership for Service-Learning objective is to move beyond preconceptions to encounter the realities of another culture.

The programs are available in the Czech Republic, Ecuador, England, France, India, Israel, Jamaica, Mexico, the Philippines, Scotland, and South Dakota. A variety of community service projects exists in each location, including teaching children and adults, working with the handicapped, literacy, community development, recreation, women's issues, and health. Program periods are summer, fall/spring, full year, and January and August intersessions. Costs range from $4400 to $8000 per semester. Most applicants are undergraduates, but anyone may apply. A one-year MA program in International Service is also offered.

International Volunteer Expeditions
2001 Vallejo Way, Sacramento, CA 95818
Tel: (916) 444-6856
Voice mail/Fax: (510) 496-2749, ext. 4550
E-mail: ivex@espwa.org   Website: www.espwa.org

International Volunteer Expeditions (IVEX) invites volunteers to assist the endeavors of organizations working for sustainable communities worldwide. The programs involve sustainability, poverty, and the environment, including agriculture and biodiversity. The type of work varies, but is primarily physical labor—construction, painting, mapping and surveying, preparing fields for farming, and trail maintenance. Some volunteers with special skills may be assigned such tasks as creating websites, researching and documenting environmental conditions, and planning educational materials. All programs are in partnership with host organizations based in the communities served. Opportunities exist throughout the Americas.

Projects last a minimum of one week and a maximum of six months; assignments may include more than one country. Volunteers pay their own transportation, incidental expenses, and a registration fee. Costs begin at $475 for six nights and all expenses are tax-deductible. Accommodations at most project sites are simple, consisting of tents, a dormitory, or the village schoolhouse. English is the working language of all IVEX projects. Technical skills are not required, but a curious, adaptable, and adventurous mind is indispensable.

Interns for Peace

475 Riverside Drive, 16th Floor, New York, NY 10115
Tel: (212) 870-2226   Fax: (212) 870-2119
E-mail: ifpus@mindspring.com
Website: www.internsforpeace.org
In Israel:
Rehove Geula 35, Tel Aviv 63304 ISRAEL
Tel: 972-3-517-6525

✒ Interns for Peace (IFP) is an independent, non-political, community-sponsored program dedicated to building trust and respect among the Jewish and Arab citizens of Israel. Guided by field staff, interns carry out the program while receiving work experience in human relations, conflict resolution, and group facilitation. Interns take on projects in education, sports, health, the arts, community and workplace relations, and adult interest groups. Basic requirements include a knowledge of and commitment to furthering Jewish-Arab relations; BA, BS, or an equivalent degree; proficiency in Hebrew or Arabic; a previous stay in Israel of at least six months; previous experience in community or human relations work; background in sports, business, teaching, health care, youth work, art, music, or community organizing. Interns are provided with housing and a monthly stipend for food, health insurance, transportation, and other daily living expenses. Interns are Jews or Arabs from Israel and abroad. Internships require a two year commitment.

Interplast, Inc.

300-B Pioneer Way, Mountain View, CA 94041-1506

Tel: (650) 962-0123   Fax: (650) 962-1619

E-mail: IPNews@interplast.org   Website: www.interplast.org

✎ Interplast is a nonprofit organization working in partnership with doctors and nurses in developing countries to provide free reconstructive surgery for children with birth defects, burns, and other crippling deformities. Interplast sends volunteer medical teams to Bolivia, Brazil, Ecuador, Honduras, Laos, Myanmar (Burma), Nepal, Peru, the Philippines, Tibet, Vietnam, and Zambia. Plastic surgeons, pediatricians, anesthesiologists, operating room nurses, and recovery nurses are needed in a volunteer capacity. Providing education and training in advanced surgical techniques and related patient care to host country medical colleagues is an important aspect of each Interplast trip; it is Interplast's goal to help each site become self-sufficient. Placements are generally two weeks. Foreign language is desirable but not required. Each trip participant pays $325 toward travel expenses.

Jesuit Volunteer Corps

PO Box 3756, Washington, DC 20007-0256

East coast: (215) 232-0300

E-mail: jvceast@jesuitvolunteers.org

Midwest: (313) 345-3480

E-mail: jvcmw@jesuitvolunteers.org

Northwest: (503) 335-8202

E-mail: jvcnw@jesuitvolunteers.org

South: (713) 756-5095

E-mail: jvcsouth@jesuitvolunteers.org

Southwest: (510) 653-8564

E-mail: jvcsw@jesuitvolunteers.org

International: (202) 687-1132
E-mail: jvi@JesuitVolunteers.org
Website: www.JesuitVolunteers.org

Each year, JVC offers about 500 men and women the opportunity to work full time for justice and peace by serving the poor directly and working for structural change. The challenge to Jesuit Volunteers (JVs) is to integrate Christian faith by working and living among the poor, living modestly in a cooperative household with other JVs, and examining the causes of social injustice. JVs serve as teachers, counselors, nurses, social workers, community organizers, and lawyers, and work with the homeless, physically and mentally ill, elderly, children, refugees, prisoners, and migrant workers. JVs serve in the US and Belize, Tanzania, Micronesia, Nepal, Peru, and Chile.

JVC welcomes women and men regardless of economic status, ethnic origin, physical challenge, marital status, or sexual orientation. Applicants must have a Christian motivation, be 21 or older, have a college degree or applicable work experience, and be without dependents. There is a particular need for applicants competent in Spanish.

Domestic placements are for one year and begin in August. International placements require a two-year commitment. JVC provides room and board, health insurance, a small personal stipend, local support teams, workshops and retreats during the year, transportation home at the end of term of service, and an active alumni association. Applications are accepted January through July with preference given to applications received before March 1.

Jewish Volunteer Corps
American Jewish World Service
989 Avenue of the Americas, 10th Floor, New York, NY 10018

Tel: (800) 889-7146 or (212) 736-2597   Fax: (212) 736-3463
E-mail: jvcvol@jws.org   Website: www.ajws.org
❧ American Jewish World Service is a nonprofit international
development agency providing non-sectarian humanitarian
assistance to communities throughout the developing world.
AJWS works exclusively with local nongovernmental
organizations in the fields of health care, sustainable
agriculture, microcredit, and education. Through the Jewish
Volunteer Corps (JVC), AJWS places professional Jewish men
and women on short term volunteer consulting assignments
with their partners in the developing world. JVC volunteers
provide technical assistance and training to the host organization while experiencing a new country and culture from the
inside.

   The International Jewish College Corps (IJCC) is a summer
program for college students that weaves together an in-depth
exploration of international development; study of Jewish texts
and traditions relating to social justice, human rights, religious
pluralism, and racial tolerance; and humanitarian service in
hands-on volunteer projects in the developing world and Israel.

Joint Assistance Center, Inc.
US Contact:
PO Box 7659, Berkeley, CA 94707-0659
Tel: (510) 464-1100   Fax: (603) 297-3521
E-mail: jacusa@juno.com
Website: jacinc.homepage.com or jacusa.homepage.com
❧ Joint Assistance Center, Inc. (JAC) is a nongovernmental
voluntary organization headquartered in Haryana State in the
outskirts of Delhi, India. It coordinates conferences and training
in various parts of India on disaster preparedness, and works in
liaison with groups, individuals, and small grassroots projects

throughout the country, focusing on such areas as community, welfare, health, education, youth development, and agricultural training. JAC welcomes volunteers from around the world to participate in the work of its partner organizations. Short term projects (minimum one month) can involve sanitation, construction, agriculture, the environment, public health, or literacy; long term projects (three months or more) are similar to the short term ones but allow for greater depth.

JAC programs run all year round. Arrangements must be made at least thirty days in advance of your arrival in India. Volunteers participate in an orientation program in New Delhi before departing for their assigned village. In New Delhi, volunteers stay at a JAC-maintained dormitory; accommodations at work camps are in homes, schools, or other public buildings. Registration fee is $50; cost for one month is $230, airfare not included. For a long term placement, the fee is $550 for the first three months and $125 for each month thereafter, airfare not included. JAC also coordinates volunteer programs with organizations in Nepal, Bangladesh, and South Korea. Send a self-addressed stamped envelope to the Berkeley address above, or follow the links from JAC's home page to find out more.

MADRE/Sisters Without Borders

121 West 27th Street, Room 301, New York, NY 10001
Tel: (212) 627-0444   Fax: (212) 675-3704
E-mail: madre@igc.org   Website: www.madre.org

🖋 MADRE places women professionals trained in midwifery, obstetrics, nutrition, sexually transmitted disease prevention, reproductive health education, drug counseling, anti-violence training, herbal medicine, and trauma counseling in Guatemala, Nicaragua, Chiapas (Mexico), Haiti, and Palestine. Volunteers provide service and conduct training workshops during short term residences at MADRE's sister organizations. Volunteers must have credentials and experience in the field in which they would like to work. Knowledge of Spanish for Central America and Chiapas and Haitian Creole or French for Haiti are required. Volunteers cover their own costs for travel and accommodation. Residencies are for approximately one to two weeks, occasionally longer.

Maryknoll Mission Association of the Faithful

PO Box 307, Maryknoll, NY 10545-0307

Tel: (800) 818-5276   Fax: (914) 762-7031

E-mail: mmaf@mkl-mmaf.org   Website: www.maryknoll.org

🖋 Maryknoll Mission Association of the Faithful (MMAF), part of the Maryknoll mission family, is a Catholic community of lay, religious, and ordained people, including families and children. MMAF members participate in the mission of Jesus, working in cross-cultural ministries in order to create a more just world in solidarity with marginalized and oppressed peoples. Missioners come from a wide range of professional and educational backgrounds and may serve in the fields of health (including direct service to persons with AIDS), education, community organizing, grassroots economic development, and formation of faith communities. MMAF has missions in Kenya, Sudan, Tanzania, Cambodia, Thailand, Vietnam, Bolivia, Brazil, Chile, El Salvador, Mexico, Peru, and Venezuela.

Mennonite Central Committee

PO Box 500, Akron, PA 17501-0500

Tel: (717) 859-1151   Fax: (717) 859-2171

E-mail: mailbox@mcc.org   Website: www.mcc.org

✎ Mennonite Central Committee (MCC) is the cooperative relief, service, and development agency of the Mennonite and Brethren in Christ churches in North America. Currently more than 800 persons serve in agriculture, health, education, social services, and community development fields in more than 50 countries including the US and Canada. Qualifications depend on assignment. Transportation, living expenses, and a small stipend are provided. MCC asks that volunteers be Christian, actively involved in a church congregation, and in agreement with MCC's nonviolent principles. Placements are for three years overseas, two years in North America.

Middle East Children's Alliance

905 Parker Street, Berkeley, CA 94710

Tel: (510) 548-0542   Fax: (510) 548-0543

E-mail: meca@peacenet.org   Website: www.mecaforpeace.org

✎ The Middle East Children's Alliance (MECA) sponsors Volunteers for Peace in Palestine, a program which places North American volunteers with Palestinian and Israeli NGOs in Jerusalem and the West Bank. Experience in areas such as health, law, agriculture, construction, or computer or English-language tutoring is useful but not required. MECA welcomes anyone who has a genuine concern for and interest in the peace process and human rights situation in Palestine and Israel, and can maintain a commitment to perform follow-up work upon returning to the US. Participants will be responsible for covering their own living expenses while abroad. Internships can vary in length from one to six months.

(Also see listing under Alternative Travel and Study Overseas)

Mission Volunteers / Overseas; Mission Volunteers / USA

Presbyterian Church (USA)

100 Witherspoon Street, Room 3409, Louisville, KY 40202-1396

Tel: (800) 779-6779

Website: www.pcusa.org/msr

🌽 The Mission Service Recruitment Office of the Presbyterian Church (USA) helps church-supported organizations and projects find full time volunteers both within the US and overseas. International assignments usually involve teaching or health care in Africa, Asia, or the Middle East. The Young Adult Volunteer Program for those 19 to 30 years of age is a one-year service-learning program at one of 12 sites in the US or internationally. Volunteers must be church affiliated. Length of service can be from three months to two years. Room and board are provided. Call for more information or visit online for an application.

Nicaragua Network

1247 E Street SE, Washington, DC 20003

Tel: (202) 544-9355   Fax: (202) 544-9359

E-mail: nicanet@afgj.org

🌽 The Network advocates for sound US foreign policies toward Nicaragua and provides information and organizing tools to a network of 200 solidarity/peace and justice committees across the United States. The Network organizes speaking tours of Nicaraguans in the US, study tours to Nicaragua, and volunteer brigades to assist in the areas of health, construction, or the environment. Two of the most important current areas of solidarity support are labor organizing in the Free Trade Zone of Managua and aid to the efforts of Nicaraguan environmental organizations.

Operation Crossroads Africa

475 Riverside Drive, Suite 1366, New York, NY 10027

Tel: (212) 870-2106   Fax: (212) 870-2644

E-mail: oca@igc.apc.org   Website: www.igc.org/oca

❧ Established in 1957, Operation Crossroads Africa oversees two volunteer programs: the Africa program, which annually supports 15 to 20 work projects in Africa, and the Diaspora program, which focuses on Brazil because of its large Afro-Brazilian population. The Crossroads summer consists of three orientation days in New York City, six weeks of service on a rural project, and one week of travel in the host country. All Crossroads ventures are community initiated, and volunteers live and work with hosts who have designed the project. Among the possible assignments are construction of community facilities, public health drives, reforestation, and teaching. Specialized skills in medicine, construction, or local languages are welcome but not necessary.

The fee for participation is $3500 exclusive of transport to and from New York. Crossroads provides fundraising advice and a limited number of partial scholarships based on need. Successful participation requires an interest in Africa and the Diaspora, strong communication skills, a desire to establish meaningful contact with people of other cultures, and a willingness to respect different beliefs and values. Many volunteers have been able to arrange academic credit for their service with Crossroads.

Peace Brigades International/USA

1904 Franklin Street, Suite 505, Oakland, CA 94612

Tel: (510) 663-2362   Fax: (510) 663-2364

E-mail: pbiusa@igc.apc.org

Website: www.igc.org/pbi/usa.html

🖋 Founded in 1981, Peace Brigades International (PBI) pioneered and practices a unique approach to the protection and promotion of human rights which has become known as "protective accompaniment." PBI fields peace teams of international volunteers trained in nonviolence to accompany individuals and organizations facing persecution as a result of their nonviolent work in defense of human rights. In addition to accompanying threatened individuals (sometimes 24 hours a day), volunteers provide workshops in peace education; maintain diplomatic relations with government, military, and police officials; report on human rights to the international community; and increase awareness of PBI's projects through public speaking tours.

Opportunities currently exist with projects in Mexico, Colombia, East Timor, and the Balkans. Prospective volunteers attend a one- to two-week training session in nonviolence before the final selections are made. Participants must be 25 years of age and commit for a minimum of one year. Volunteers for Mexico or Colombia must be fluent in Spanish; for the Balkans, English; for East Timor, Indonesian is preferred but not required.

Peacework
305 Washington Street SW, Blacksburg, VA 24060-4745
Tel: (540) 953-1376   Fax: (540) 552-0119
E-mail: mail@peacework.org   Website: www.peacework.org
🖋 Peacework manages short term volunteer service projects around the world in cooperation with indigenous relief and development organizations. Projects can be arranged for college, university, and community service organizations as well as individuals. Orientation and interaction with the host community is a vital part of the program, in addition to the assistance which volunteers provide in building houses, schools, health

facilities, and other projects with the poor. International experience, building skills, volunteer service, and foreign language
proficiency are helpful but not required. Anyone with a genuine
interest in global service is invited to participate. Project locations change each year and have been offered in places such as
Vietnam, Russia, Mexico, Zimbabwe, Honduras, the Dominican
Republic, Belize, Nicaragua, Costa Rica, and the United States.
Typical costs range from $500 to $900 plus airfare. Limited
scholarships are available. Contact Peacework for information
about annual projects, dates, and costs.

Plenty International

PO Box 394, Summertown, TN 38483
Tel/Fax: (931) 964-4864
E-mail: plenty1@usit.net   Website: www.plenty.org
🌶 Founded in 1974, Plenty promotes the exchange of appropriate village-scale technologies, skills, and resources between
people worldwide in a spirit of cooperation, friendship, and
mutual respect. Special focus is on indigenous peoples and environmental protection. Projects are based primarily in Central
America, Dominica, Liberia, and two Native American reservations in the US. Volunteers pay their own travel and living
expenses. Long term volunteers (three months or more) with
skills in organic agriculture, primary health care, sustainable
energy, small business, and computers are preferred. Send a
SASE for a listing of current volunteer opportunities.

Quest
(See listing under US Voluntary Service Organizations)

Service Civil International
814 NE 40th Street, Seattle, WA 98105

Tel/Fax: (206) 545-6585

E-mail: sciinfo@sci-ivs.org   Website: www.sci-ivs.org

⚘ Service Civil International (SCI) organizes work camps in the US, Latin America, Europe, Asia, and Africa to promote cross-cultural understanding and international peace. Volunteers work on environmental, construction, solidarity, and social service projects and live together in simple quarters for two to three weeks. Volunteers must be 16 or older for US work camps, 18 or older for European camps, and at least 21 with SCI work camp experience for projects in Africa, Asia, or Latin America. Volunteers pay travel expenses and a small fee; SCI covers room, board, and accident insurance. Many work camps are accessible to disabled people. Application fees are $125 for overseas and $65 for US camps.

Servicio Internacional para la Paz/International Service for Peace (SIPAZ)

PO Box 2415, Santa Cruz, CA 95063

Tel/Fax: (831) 425-1257

E-mail: admin@sipaz.org   Website: www.sipaz.org

⚘ Organized at the invitation of Mexican church and human rights groups, SIPAZ is a coalition of North American, Latin American, and European organizations dedicated to supporting the peace process in Chiapas. SIPAZ seeks long term volunteers to help carry out its work. Tasks include developing and maintaining relationships with groups and individuals concerned in the conflict, monitoring both formal talks and independent initiatives, preparing updates and analysis on the ongoing peace process, designing workshops on nonviolence, and assisting with presence and accompaniment duties. Prospective volunteers must be fluent in Spanish, 23 years or older, and have prior international work experience. Candidates should be committed to nonviolence and comfortable working with faith-based groups. A commitment of at least one year is required.

Toledo Eco-Tourism Association and Punta Gorda Conservation Committee

Box 45, Punta Gorda, BELIZE

Tel: 501-07-22119

E-mail: ttea@btl.net

🌿 The Toledo Eco-Tourism Association (TEA) works with fourteen indigenous communities (thirteen Maya and one Garifuna) in the areas of eco-tourism, rainforest conservation, and sustainable development. The association has been active since 1990. Founded in 1996, the Punta Gorda Conservation Committee (PGCC) is an urban group seeking to establish eco-tourist sites on what remains of the public land around Punta Gorda. The sites will be run by and for the benefit of local people. Volunteers have worked as instructors in training for office operation, trail development, guide training, arts and crafts development, grant-writing, and media.

A major current project is the establishment of community conservation areas for nineteen villages for which a grant is pending with UNDP. Volunteers must cover all expenses, including transportation, and room and board at an average of $20 per day or $400 per month. Belizeans speak English. The average length of stay for volunteers has been two to three months but a longer stay is possible.

Visions in Action

2710 Ontario Road NW, Washington, DC 20009

Tel: (202) 625-7402   Fax: (202) 625-2353

E-mail: visions@igc.org   Website: www.visionsinaction.org

🍂 Visions in Action arranges for volunteers to work in urban
and rural areas of Africa and Latin America with development
organizations and the media. Placements are made for one
year in Uganda, Tanzania, Zimbabwe, and Burkina Faso, and
for six or twelve months in Liberia, South Africa, or Mexico.
Placements include project management, health care, journal-
ism, youth group organizing, research and writing, human
rights, democracy, housing, microfinancing, and community
development. All participants take part in a one month orientation that includes intensive language training, cross-cultural
awareness, and field trips to development projects. An additional purpose of the program is to educate people in the US
about Third World countries through volunteers' published articles and slide show or videotape presentations given to schools
and groups upon return to the US. Most volunteers live in
group houses with other volunteers. Volunteers pay for their
own expenses, which average $4500 to $6000 including airfare.
All volunteers receive a small monthly stipend.

Voluntarios Solidarios
Fellowship of Reconciliation
Task Force on Latin America and the Caribbean
2017 Mission Street, #305, San Francisco, CA 94110
Tel: (415) 495-6334   Fax: (415) 495-5628
E-mail: forlatam@igc.org   Website: www.nonviolence.org
🍂 Voluntarios Solidarios places volunteers with Latin American
and Caribbean groups engaged in nonviolence education,
human rights documentation, and advocacy efforts with the
regions' poor majority. Each volunteer's work is shaped by the
needs of the host organization. Common needs include transla-
tion of publications, support of peace actions, technical
assistance in carpentry, computer operation, recycling,

assistance with human welfare service, children and elderly care
projects, and conflict resolution. Volunteers must be self-
funded, at least 21 years old, and functional in Spanish. Length
of placements range from three months to two years.

Volunteers for Peace, Inc.

1034 Tiffany Road, Belmont, VT 05730

Tel: (802) 259-2759   Fax: (802) 259-2922

E-mail: vfp@vfp.org   Website: www.vfp.org

🖋 Volunteers for Peace (VFP) recruits volunteers for over
1500 work camps in 70 different countries. At a work camp,
ten to twenty people from five or more countries join together
for two to three weeks to support community projects in construction, restoration, environmental work, social services,
agriculture, and archaeology. In 1999, VFP exchanged over
1300 volunteers. Volunteers arrange their own travel and pay
a registration fee of $200 which covers room and board for
the duration of most programs. Volunteers can participate in
multiple camps in the same or different countries. Call, write,
or email VFP for a free newsletter which includes many
reports and photos from their programs.

Volunteers in Asia

PO Box 20266, Stanford, CA 94309

Tel: (650) 723-3228   Fax: (650) 725-1805

E-mail: volasia@volasia.org   Website: www.volasia.org

🖋 At the request of Asian institutions, Volunteers in Asia (VIA)
places undergraduates and recent graduates in teaching and
English resource positions in China, Indonesia, Vietnam, and
Laos. Applicants must attend a three-month part time preparation and training program at Stanford University prior to
placement. Volunteers pay an initial fee of $1,350 for a one year

placement or $950 for a two-year placement. This fee covers insurance, training costs, and round-trip air fare. The host institution provides an in-country stipend for basic living expenses.

Volunteers in Mission

4503 Broadway, San Antonio, TX 78209

Tel: (210) 828-2224   Fax: (210) 828-9741

E-mail: geranio20@hotmail.com

🌶 Volunteers in Mission (VIM) seeks a new economic, social, and political order that promotes justice and solidarity. Volunteers work with homeless women and children, do pastoral work, teach in US/Mexico border schools and in the Sierra Tarahumara, and provide preventive health care. Programs are organized in both the US and Mexico. Volunteers must be at least 21 years old, single or married with no dependents, and commit to one year in the US or two to three years in Mexico. If volunteering in Mexico, they should be Catholic. Volunteers pay cost of transportation to the orientation site and language school if needed. All other costs, like medical insurance, are paid by VIM.

Volunteer Missionary Movement

5980 West Loomis Road, Greendale, WI 53129

Tel: (414) 423-8660

E-mail: vmm@execpc.com

Website: www.execpc.com/~vmm/index.html

🌶 The Volunteer Missionary Movement (VMM) is an international community of Christians with its origins in Catholic tradition. Established in 1969, VMM is the first and only international lay mission organization founded and democratically operated by laity. VMM missioners proclaim the Good News by sharing lives, resources, and skills with those in need, and thus challenge oppressive and unjust structures and promote equality, respect, and dignity for all. VMM maintains mission projects in Guatemala, El Salvador, Kenya, Uganda, Zimbabwe, Zambia, South Africa, Mexico, and the United States.

Volunteers should possess knowledge of Christ and a commitment to live in Christian community, willingness to live simply, openness to an ecumenical mission perspective, sensitivity and respect for others, flexibility, and a sense of humor. Work experience and/or specific skills are necessary; a college degree is preferred but not required. Volunteers should commit for two years. Placement of families is possible. Positions open include teaching, construction, community organizing, and grant writing for host country NGOs.

Witness for Peace

1229 15th Street NW, Washington, DC 20005
Tel: (202) 588-1471   Fax: (202) 588-1472
E-mail: witness@witnessforpeace.org
Website: www.witnessforpeace.org

ò Volunteers with Witness for Peace (WFP) work with communities in Nicaragua, Guatemala, Chiapas, and Cuba, making a two year commitment. Long term volunteers document human rights abuses, study the effects of North American foreign and economic policies on the region, provide socio-political analyses of domestic affairs, facilitate short term delegations of North Americans, and stand with the people in the spirit of international awareness and the ethos of nonviolence as a means for positive social change. Volunteers must be US citizens and fluent in Spanish. Volunteers pay costs of round-trip airfare and attempt to raise $1,000 for WFP to help cover living expenses. WFP provides training, room and board, medical, and a monthly stipend. WFP is an interfaith organization.

WorldTeach, Inc.

Center for International Development
Harvard University
79 John F. Kennedy Street, Cambridge, MA 02138
Tel: 1-800-4-TEACH-0 or (617) 495-5527   Fax: (617) 495-1599
E-mail: info@worldteach.org   Website: www.worldteach.org

✎ WorldTeach is a private, nonprofit organization based at the
Center for International Development at Harvard University.
Founded in 1986, WorldTeach provides opportunities for individuals to make a meaningful contribution to international
education while living and working as volunteer teachers in
developing countries. Volunteers teach English for one year or
six months to students of a variety of ages depending on the
country. Currently, teachers are needed in Costa Rica, China,
Ecuador, Namibia, and Honduras. A bachelor's degree is
required for long term teaching assignments. Some summer
assignments are available in Yantai, China which are open to
all individuals 18 years of age or older. No previous language
or teaching experience is necessary.

Housing is provided during the period of service, and
volunteers pay a fee covering direct expenses such as international airfare, insurance, training and orientation, and
in-country staff support. Volunteers receive a small monthly
living allowance during the course of their service. Student
loans may be deferred while volunteers serve. Applications
are accepted on a rolling admissions basis, and may be printed
from the WorldTeach website or requested by contacting the
WorldTeach admissions office.

US VOLUNTARY
SERVICE ORGANIZATIONS

WORKING OVERSEAS IS not the only way to gain community development experience. In many areas of the US, people face conditions of poverty similar to those found in the Third World. Voluntary service in the US can offer a low cost opportunity for building solid credentials towards a career in community development.

One of the best resources for domestic volunteering may well be your local Yellow Pages, under Social Service Organizations. Here are some organizations that recruit nationally and perform admirable work.

ACORN
88 Third Avenue, Brooklyn, NY 11217
Tel: (718) 246-7900   Fax: (718) 246-7939
E-mail: fielddirect@acorn.org   Website: www.acorn.org
♪ ACORN (Association of Community Organizations for Reform Now) is a neighborhood-based, multi-racial membership organization of low income families working to gain power within institutions that affect their everyday lives. Volunteers work as grassroots organizers throughout the US. They receive a salary and must commit to one year of service. A working knowledge of Spanish and previous organizing experience are preferred, but not required.

Amizade, Ltd.
(See listing under International Voluntary Service Organizations)

67

Bike-Aid
(See listing under Alternative Travel and Study Overseas)

Bikes Not Bombs
(See listing under International Voluntary Service Organizations)

Brethren Volunteer Services
(See listing under International Voluntary Service Organizations)

Buddhist Alliance for Social Engagement (BASE)
PO Box 4650, Berkeley, CA 94704

Tel: (510) 655-6169   Fax: (510) 655-1369

E-mail: bpf@bpf.org   Website: www.bpf.org/base.html

🍂 BASE is a program of the Buddhist Peace Fellowship, begun in the San Francisco Bay Area in 1995. BASE provides a structure for a group of volunteers to spend six months in service/social change work combined with intensive Buddhist practice. Placements include work in soup kitchens, shelters, hospices, urban community garden projects, and social justice organizations. Those volunteering 30 hours a week are offered a modest stipend and housing.

BASE volunteers meet regularly for study of Engaged Buddhism, meditation, and discussion and support. Applicants must have service, group, and meditation experience. In addition to Bay Area BASE groups, the program has expanded to include groups in Boston, Massachusetts; Boulder, Colorado; and Santa Cruz and Arcata, California.

Catholic Worker Movement
125 locations throughout the US; for a copy of or subscription to the Catholic Worker newspaper, please contact:

The Catholic Worker

36 East First Street, New York, NY 10003

Website: www.catholicworker.org

♪ Founded by Dorothy Day and Peter Maurin in 1933, the
Catholic Worker Movement is grounded in the firm belief of
the God-given dignity of every person. CW Communities are
committed to nonviolence, voluntary poverty, and hospitality
for the homeless, exiled, hungry, and forsaken. Houses are
independent of one another and vary in their activities, relationship to the Catholic Church, and how they incorporate Catholic
Worker philosophy and tradition. Most are based on the
Gospel, prayer, and Catholic beliefs, but some are interfaith.
There is no national Catholic Worker headquarters. Catholic
Workers live a simple lifestyle in community, serve the poor,
and resist war and social injustice. Most houses need volunteers; contact the house you are interested in directly for
further information. The national CW website maintains a
complete list of community houses.

Center for Third World Organizing

1218 East 21st Street, Oakland, CA 94606

Tel: (510) 533-7583   Fax: (510) 533-0923

E-mail: training@ctwo.org   Website: www.ctwo.org

♪ The Center for Third World Organizing (CTWO) is a
research and training center working on issues affecting Third
World communities in the US. Its apprenticeship program for
minority activists provides training and field experience for
young people of color who are involved in work for social
change. Each summer and fall, this seven-week program trains
people (primarily college students) in the techniques of community organizing. Volunteers receive housing and a stipend.
Other internships are sometimes available, including research
and writing for the Center newsletter.

Christian Peacemaker Teams
(See listing under International Voluntary Service Organizations)

Episcopal Urban Internship Program
260 North Locust Street, Inglewood, CA 90301

Tel: (310) 674-7700   Fax: (310) 674-7181

E-mail: euip@pacbell.net   Website: www.euip.org

✎ The Episcopal Urban Internship Program is a one-year voluntary service program for young adults (ages 21 to 30). Interns are placed with urban social service organizations within the Los Angeles area and live communally in a house in Inglewood. In addition to their job placements, the interns are expected to play an active role in their household community and to take part in the life of the sponsoring Episcopal parish. Individuals do not need to be Episcopalians to be urban interns. The program provides a monthly stipend, along with health insurance and housing. Participants are eligible for an AmeriCorps grant upon completion of year. Additional benefits include quarterly retreats and weekly theological reflection times.

Food First (Institute for Food and Development Policy)
(See description of Food First at the back of this book)

Fourth World Movement
(See listing under International Voluntary Service Organizations)

Global Citizens Network
(See listing under Alternative Travel and Study Overseas)

Global Routes
(See listing under International Voluntary Service Organizations)

Habitat for Humanity International
(See listing under International Voluntary Service Organizations)

Heifer Project International
1015 South Louisiana Street, Little Rock, AR 72202
Tel: (800) 422-0474 or (501) 376-6836   Fax: (501) 376-8906
E-mail: info@heifer.org   Website: www.heifer.org
Heifer Project International (HPI) is a worldwide community development organization that provides farm animals, as
well as training and related agricultural and community-building services, to farmers in developing areas in 44 countries,
including the US. The program offers volunteer opportunities at
its International Learning and Livestock Center, its national
office in Arkansas, and its organic farm in Massachusetts. HPI
also conducts eight- to ten-day study tours in countries where it
has programs. Groups learn about development issues and may
help build facilities for HPI projects. Volunteers pay their own
expenses, which usually range from $1000 to $3000.

The International Partnership for Service-Learning
(See listing under International Voluntary Service Organizations)

International Volunteer Expeditions
(See listing under International Voluntary Service Organizations)

Jesuit Volunteer Corps
(See listing under International Voluntary Service Organizations)

Lutheran Volunteer Corps

1226 Vermont Avenue, NW, Washington, DC 20005

Tel: (202) 387-3222   Fax: (202) 667-0037

E-mail: staff@lvchome.org   Website: www.lvchome.org

✦ Lutheran Volunteer Corps volunteers work in direct service, public policy, advocacy, community organizing, and education. Placements are in Baltimore, MD; Wilmington, DE; Washington, DC; Chicago, IL; Milwaukee, WI; Minneapolis/St. Paul, MN; and Seattle, WA. Volunteers live communally with three to six other volunteers. Travel, room and board, medical coverage, and daily work-related transportation expenses are covered. The program is open to people of all faiths. Contact Joanne Roepke Bode, Recruitment Coordinator.

Mennonite Voluntary Service

PO Box 347, 722 Main Street, Newton, KS 67117-0347

Tel: (316) 283-5100   Fax: (316) 283-0454

E-mail: mvs@gcmc.org

Website: www2.southwind.net/~gcmc

✦ Mennonite Voluntary Service (MVS) helps meet the needs of poor and disadvantaged people in the US and Canada. Volunteer placements range from staffing food banks and emergency assistance centers to working with after school programs. Social work, community organization, housing rehabilitation, and education skills are in particular demand. Initial terms of two years are strongly encouraged, though some assignments are available for one year. Spanish is helpful or required for some positions. Volunteers must be Christian, at least 20 years old, and from the US or Canada. All expenses are covered by MVS.

Mission Volunteers/USA

(See listing under International Voluntary Service Organizations)

Passionist Lay Missioners

5700 North Harlem Avenue, Chicago, IL 60631-2342

Tel: (773) 631-6336   Fax: (773) 631-8059

E-mail: plm@visioni.com   Website: www.passionist.org/plm

Passionist Lay Missioners (PLM) are volunteers who seek to address immediate and systemic problems of poverty by working with economically disadvantaged and disenfranchised people in Chicago, Detroit, and San Antonio. Positions begin in August and last for one year or more, and include social workers, youth workers, advocates for the homeless, teachers and teacher's aides, emergency intervention workers, community organizers, peace and justice advocates, prisoners' rights advocates, child care workers, counselors, domestic violence workers, clerical workers, caregivers for the elderly, legal aides, and more. Volunteers live in community in low income, inner city neighborhoods. They live a simple lifestyle and explore connections between work, community, faith, and social justice.

Room and board, health insurance, a monthly stipend of $100, and a $300 transition stipend at the completion of the program are provided. Volunteers pay their own transportation to the orientation in August. Applicants must be 21 years or older, have practical work experience or some college education, and be willing to engage in spiritual reflection. PLM is a part of the AmeriCorps through Catholic Network of Volunteer Service. Missioners can join through PLM and receive loan deferment and an educational award of $4725.

Plenty International

(See listing under International Voluntary Service Organizations)

Proyecto Libertad

113 North 1st Street, Harlingen, TX 78550

Tel: (956) 425-9552   Fax: (956) 425-8249

➷ Proyecto Libertad (PL) is a legal office on the Texas-Mexico border representing immigrants. PL provides legal services, help in applying for political asylum and other forms of immigration relief, and advocacy for immigrants (including minors) in detention. They also raise bond money and contact relatives. PL also participates in federal litigation to protect immigrant rights. Volunteers work on all aspects of the program, must speak Spanish and be sensitive to multicultural differences. Volunteers pay their own expenses, but some assistance may be available.

Quest

3706 Rhode Island Avenue, Mt. Rainier, MD 20712
Tel: (301) 277-2514
E-mail: info@quest-rjm.org   Website: www.quest-rjm.org

➷ Quest, a volunteer program sponsored by the Religious of Jesus and Mary, offers year-long and summer opportunities in the Bronx, NY; Los Angeles, CA; Washington, DC; Tijuana, Mexico; and Haiti. Volunteers share simple living in Christian community while daily serving the poor in education, medical work, community development, AIDS ministry, homeless shelters, and clinics. Orientation, room, board, medical insurance, monthly stipend, retreats, and daily transportation are provided. Volunteers must provide their own transportation at the beginning and end of the term. Volunteers are eligible for an AmeriCorps Education Award.

Service Civil International

(See listing under International Voluntary Service Organizations)

Sioux Indian YMCA

PO Box 218, Dupree, SD 57623

Tel: (605) 365-5232

🖊 Volunteers of college age or older serve for two months during the summer as camp staff at Leslie Marrowbone Memorial YMCA Camp, working with eight- to fourteen-year-old Sioux children. Also needed are community work volunteers to live in small, isolated Sioux communities to support various youth and family projects. These placements are for nine to twelve months. Volunteers must have camp or community work skills, and be flexible and able to share their own cultures, as well as relate to others. The YMCA can help with room and board.

United Farm Workers

PO Box 62, La Paz, Keene, CA 93531

Tel: (661) 823-6252   Fax: (661) 823-6177

E-mail: jruiz@ufwmail.org   Website: www.ufw.org

🖊 United Farm Workers (UFW) works for justice for farm workers and safe food for consumers. UFW is seeking staff who can spend one year or more in rural or urban areas, organizing farm workers and consumers. Opportunities are also available in administrative capacities. Staff receive between $750 to $1500 depending on experience.

Volunteer Missionary Movement

(See listing under International Voluntary Service Organizations)

Witness for Peace

(See listing under International Voluntary Service Organizations)

ALTERNATIVE TRAVEL AND STUDY OVERSEAS

IN THIS SECTION you will find shorter-term volunteer opportunities as well as options for travel to unusual destinations. A brief work stint with one of the organizations listed here (say a two-week excursion building a well in Nicaragua with El Porvenir) can acquaint you with living in poor countries and help you decide if a long term commitment makes sense for you. A number of groups conduct "reality tours," study tours, or delegations in the Third World and the US. These are socially responsible educational tours that provide participants with firsthand experience of the political, economic, and social structures that create or sustain hunger, poverty, and environmental degradation. Tour participants meet with people from diverse sectors with various perspectives on issues of agriculture, development, and the environment. They often stay with local people, visit rural areas, and meet with grassroots organizers. The experience and insights gained on such a tour may influence participants' future work for democratic social change.

Many universities offer study-abroad programs. This section mentions just a few of these.

African American Studies Program
PO Box 497327, Chicago, IL 60649
Tel: (773) 667-1285   Fax: (773) 684-6967
♪ The African American Studies Program offers a variety of study tours throughout Africa. Past tour themes have included economic and political development of states and the role

of women in the family. Tours are led by scholars of African studies.

Bicycle Africa

International Bicycle Fund
4887 Columbia Drive South, #Q, Seattle, WA 98108-1919
Tel/Fax: (206) 767-0848
E-mail: ibike@ibike.org   Website:www.ibike.org
🖎 The International Bicycle Fund (IBF) arranges two- to four-week cultural and educational bicycle tours in the US, Cuba, Cameroon, Kenya, Uganda, Tanzania, Tunisia, Malawi, Eritrea, Ethiopia, Mali, Senegal, Gambia, Ghana, Togo, Benin, Burkina Faso, South Africa, Zimbabwe, and other African countries. Specialists accompany groups to areas seldom visited by Westerners. Cycling is moderate and participants do not need to have extensive touring experience. Costs range from $900 to $2500, not including airfare. The International Bicycle Fund promotes bicycle transportation, economic development, international understanding, and safety education.

Bike-Aid

JustAct—Youth Action for Global Justice
333 Valencia Street, Suite 101, San Francisco, CA 94103-3547
Tel: (415) 431-4480   Fax: (415) 431-5953
E-mail: info@justact.org
Websites: www.bikeaid.org, www.justact.org
🖎 Bike-Aid is an innovative cross-country cycling adventure sponsored by JustAct (Youth ACTion for Global JUSTice). JustAct works to develop in young people a lifelong commitment to social and economic justice around the world. JustAct provides a network linking students and youth to educational opportunities and to grassroots movements working for

equitable, sustainable, and self-reliant communities locally and globally. Bike-Aid combines physical challenge, community interaction, global education, leadership, fundraising, and service learning into the empowering experience of a lifetime. Every summer 85 individuals from around the world cycle along four different routes, starting in Portland, Oregon; San Francisco, California; Seattle, Washington; and Montreal, Canada, ending up in Washington, DC at the end of the summer. Along the routes, participants exchange information and get a firsthand look into local community groups, the issues that are facing them, and the solutions that are taking place. Overnight lodging includes organic farms, Native American Indian reservations, churches, and camping in some of the most beautiful spots the US has to offer.

Beginners to prize-winning racers have participated in Bike-Aid, and riders from the ages of 16 to 60 have met the challenge. It is not a race, and JustAct encourages the participation of people from all backgrounds, ages, and abilities. Cyclists must be willing to live in a community throughout the summer, and intern/volunteers must be resourceful and able to work in a team environment.

Center for Global Education
Augsburg College
2211 Riverside Avenue, Minneapolis, MN 55454
Tel: (800) 299-8889 or (612) 330-1159   Fax: (612) 330-1695
E-mail: globaled@augsburg.edu
Website: www.augsburg.edu/global
🕊 The Center for Global Education designs and coordinates travel seminars to Central America, Mexico, the Caribbean, and Southern Africa. The goal is to foster critical analysis of local and global conditions so that personal and systemic change

takes place. Participants meet with a wide range of representatives in government and business, church, and grassroots communities. Focus is on sustainable development, human rights, women's roles, and the role and responsibility of people in working for social change. The Center's programs are utilized by a wide variety of civic groups, churches, colleges, and individuals. They also arrange longer study programs for undergraduate students.

Christian Peacemaker Teams
(See listing under International Voluntary Service Organizations)

Co-op America Travel-Links
120 Beacon Street, Somerville, MA 02143
Tel: (800) 648-2667 or in MA (617) 497-8163
Fax: (617) 492-3720
E-mail: mj@tvlcoll.com
🌢 Travel-Links is a full service travel agency that emphasizes responsible tourism and seeks to promote understanding and cooperation among people through non-exploitative travel. Make your travel dollars count.

Cristianos por la Paz in El Salvador (CRISPAZ)
(See listing under International Voluntary Service Organizations)

Cultural Restoration Tourism Project
c/o Mark A. Hintzke
722A Liggett Avenue, San Francisco, CA 94129
Tel: (415) 563-7221
E-mail: crtp@earthlink.net
Website: home.earthlink.net/~crtp/

🌢 In Mongolia in the summer of 1999, the Cultural Restoration Tourism Project (CRTP) began the restoration of the Baldan Baraivan temple, built in the 1700s, badly damaged in the 1930s by the Soviet regime, and one of the few standing Buddhist monasteries of its kind. Through the use of volunteer tourism, CRTP will fund and execute the restoration of the main temple. Tours are available to the general public each summer through the project's completion, currently scheduled for 2005. Volunteers do not need any construction experience, just a will and desire to see the temple rebuilt. Local community members will be employed full time and volunteers will work alongside Mongolian staff. Participants will stay in traditional yurts, each of which houses two to three people. Opportunities for overnights in the wilderness will be available; travelers should bring their own tents if interested in camping or desiring private accommodations.

Earthwatch

3 Clock Tower Place, Suite 100, Box 75, Maynard, MA 01754
Tel: (800) 776-0188 or (978) 461-0081   Fax: (978) 461-2332
E-mail: info@earthwatch.org   Website: www.earthwatch.org
🌢 Earthwatch sponsors scholarly field research using volunteers to help scientists on research expeditions around the world. Most of the projects undertake to study endangered ecosystems, biodiversity, and resource management, but a handful each year center on public health and sustainable development. For example, in 1998, volunteers worked with Ohio University's Dr. Prisca Nemapare in her study of maternal and child health in the Masvingo province of Zimbabwe or helped former Peace Corps volunteer and nurse Phyllis Jansyn in her work to eliminate intestinal parasites in Cameroon. Each of these projects lasts two weeks. Project contributions

range from $700 to $4000 and do not include airfare to the
research site.

El Porvenir

2508 42nd Street, Sacramento, CA 95817
Tel: (916) 736-3663   Fax: (916) 227-5068
E-mail: info@elporvenir.org   Website: www.elporvenir.org
❧ El Porvenir supports sustainable infrastructure development
in poor rural communities in Nicaragua through funding and
technical aid to locally originated potable water, sanitation, and
reforestation projects. El Porvenir sponsors two-week work
trips and one-week educational tours to Nicaragua twice a year.
The cost of the educational tour is $950 per person plus airfare
to Nicaragua; the cost of the work tour is $650 plus airfare.
Work tour participants stay in family homes or other simple
lodging and assist with a construction project. Educational
tours, limited in size to ten persons, visit various El Porvenir
project villages and engage in cultural and recreational activities. No Spanish is required, and no construction experience
is required for the work tour.

Explorations in Travel, Inc.

1922 River Road, Guilford, VT 05301
Tel: (802) 257-0152   Fax: (802) 257-2784
E-mail: explore@volunteertravel.com
Website: www.volunteertravel.com
❧ Explorations in Travel provides volunteer work placements
for students and adults from all over the world. Placements can
be arranged in Belize, Costa Rica, Ecuador, Mexico, Nepal,
Puerto Rico, and Samoa (as well as Australia and New Zealand).
Work sites include, but are not limited to, schools, conservation
areas, wildlife rehabilitation centers, rainforests, farms, and

eco-tourism reserves. Language classes can be incorporated into
a placement. Fees range from $750 to $950; there is a non-
refundable application fee of $35. Both individual and group
programs are available. Explorations in Travel can also help
with flight arrangements and fundraising ideas.

Global Citizens Network

130 North Howell Street, St. Paul, MN 55104
Tel: (800) 644-9292 or (651) 644-0960
E-mail: gcn@mtn.org   Website: www.globalcitizens.org

🌱 Global Citizens Network (GCN) offers individuals the
opportunity to interact with people of diverse cultures in
order to develop creative and effective local solutions to global
problems. GCN sends short term teams of volunteers to communities in other cultures. Each team is partnered with a
grassroots organization active in meeting community needs.
Volunteers assist and work under the direction of local people
on locally-initiated projects, staying with host families or living
as a group at a community center. Each team member receives
training materials and participates in an orientation session.
Groups are led by GCN team leaders; a local resident serves
as translator and language tutor.

Tours last one to three weeks including travel time. Program
costs run from $550 to $1650, airfare not included. Expenses
are tax deductible in the United States. No specific skills are
required. There are no upper age restrictions; underage volunteers must be accompanied by a parent or guardian. Past
destinations have included Guatemala, Belize, Nepal, Kenya,
Bolivia, the Yucatan, and Native reservations in Arizona, South
Dakota, and New Mexico. Tasks range from school or road
repair, water and sanitation projects, to trail renovation.

Global Exchange

2017 Mission Street, Suite 303, San Francisco, CA 94110

Tel: (415) 255-7296   Fax: (415) 255-7498

E-mail: info@globalexchange.org Website: www.globalexchange.org

✎ Global Exchange organizes reality tours, study seminars,
and human rights delegations to more than 25 countries. These
study tours offer a unique opportunity to learn firsthand
about pressing issues confronting the Third World. Tour participants meet with peasant and labor organizers, community and
religious leaders, peace activists, environmentalists, scholars,
students, indigenous leaders, and government officials.
Countries visited include South Africa, Zimbabwe, Cuba, Haiti,
Iran, Mexico (Chiapas and the US-Mexico border), Central
America, Vietnam, Northern Ireland, Ecuador, and Brazil. Costs
range from $800 to $3200. Global Exchange also offers Spanish
language, dance, and bicycle trips to Cuba, and opportunities
for volunteer work related to human rights in Mexico.

Heifer Project International

(See listing under US Voluntary Service Organizations)

IFCO/Pastors for Peace

(See listing under International Voluntary Service Organizations)

Institute for Central American Development Studies (ICADS)

Dept. 826, PO Box 025216, Miami, FL 33102-5216

E-mail: icads@netbox com   Website: www.icadscr.com

In Costa Rica:

Apartado 3 (2070), Sabanilla, San Jose, COSTA RICA

Tel: 011-506-225-0508   Fax: 011-506-234-1337

🖋 The Institute for Central American Development Studies
(ICADS) is a nonprofit center for research and analysis of
Central American social and environmental issues. Four study
and internship programs are offered. The first is a study-
abroad/internship semester for undergrads combining four
weeks of course work in Central American social topics and
Spanish with a two-month internship with NGOs in Costa
Rica, Nicaragua, or Panama. Students return to ICADS in Costa
Rica for written work and oral presentations at the end of their
internship. The second is the 14-week Field Course in Resource
Management and Sustainable Development, also for undergrads, which includes four weeks of intensive Spanish and
urban studies, five weeks of group travel in the field, and five
weeks of independent research. For undergrads, graduates, and
professionals interested in Costa Rica, ICADS has a non-credit
Summer Internship program comprising three weeks of Spanish
study and seven weeks of intern service. ICADS also offers
intensive Spanish language courses every month except
December for students 18 years and up.

Juan Sisay Escuela de Español
c/o Yaneth Gramajo
15 Avenida 8-38 Zona 1, Quetzaltenango, GUATEMALA
Tel: 011-502-765-1318 (school office)
or 011-502-761-1586 (weekends and evenings)
Fax: 011-502-763-2104
(be sure to write "Juan Sisay Escuela" on fax cover)
E-mail: Jsisayxela@c.net.gt
Website: www.xelapages.com/juansisay or www.juansisay.de
US contact:
Matt Foster, 98 Church Street #1, Mountain View, CA 94041
E-mail: mfoster@area.com

❧ Founded in 1989, Escuela Juan Sisay is a nonprofit educational collective for intensive instruction in the Spanish language. The language courses consist of one-on-one instruction for five hours a day, Monday through Friday. All the teachers are university educated and trained in language teaching. The individualized instruction allows teachers to structure classes to meet the specific language interests and needs of each student, from beginning to advanced speakers. As part of the school's total immersion program, students can be placed with Guatemalan host families, providing additional language practice. In addition to language classes, students can participate in optional enrichment activities including lectures and movies about Guatemalan history and culture, field trips to local places of interest, and any of several community projects. These projects include a reforestation effort in the hills around Quetzaltenango, an educational scholarship program for local families, and weekly English classes for children attending public school.

Tuition costs are $125 per week except between June 1 and August 15 when the cost is $140 per week. This tuition includes 25 hours of instruction, room and three meals per day with a Guatemalan family, and a certificate of studies completed. The school also offers a free pick-up service for students upon arrival at the airport or bus station.

Los Niños

287 "G" Street, Chula Vista, CA 91910
Tel: (619) 426-9110   Fax: (619) 426-6664
E-mail: losninos@home.com

❧ Los Niños supports long term community development projects in Tijuana, Mexicali, and San Diego. Programs include agriculture, nutrition, organic gardening, and development education, and are designed to promote self-reliance and social awareness. Los Niños offers weekend and week-long tour/seminar/work project programs to US students who want to learn more about community development through hands-on participation. Cost varies according to length of stay. Los Niños is not religiously or politically affiliated in any way.

Marazul Tours, Inc.

Tower Plaza Mall, 4100 Park Avenue, Weehawken, NJ 07087
Tel: 800-223-5334 or (201) 840-6711   Fax: (201) 840-6719
E-mail: info@marazultours.com
Website: www.marazultours.com

🌿 Marazul Tours is a well-known coordinator of alternative tours to Central America. Many of the organizations in this guide enlist Marazul's expertise in planning trips to Cuba, El Salvador, Guatemala, and Nicaragua. Marazul is a progressive full service travel agency and contributes one percent of the price of your airline ticket to many socially responsible groups through its "Fly With Your Commitment" program.

Middle East Children's Alliance

905 Parker Street, Berkeley, CA 94710
Tel: (510) 548-0542   Fax: (510) 548-0543
E-mail: meca@peacenet.org   Website: www.peacenet.org/meca

🌿 The Middle East Children's Alliance raises funds for humanitarian aid (medical supplies, school books, food, and clothing) for children in Iraq and the West Bank in Gaza. They sponsor short term delegations several times a year to Palestine and Israel. These delegates meet with Israeli peace activists and visit Palestinian production cooperatives, refugee camps, health clinics, and kindergartens in the West Bank and Gaza. Costs of programs vary. The Middle East Children's Alliance supports the establishment of a viable Palestinian state alongside Israel.

(See listing under International Voluntary Service Organizations)

Minnesota Studies in International Development

University of Minnesota, 102 Nicholson Hall, 216 Pillsbury Drive
SE, Minneapolis, MN 55455-0138
Tel: (612) 626-9000   Fax: (612) 626-8009
E-mail: Umabroad@umn.edu
Website: www.Umabroad.umn.edu

🍃 Minnesota Studies in International Development (MSID) combines intensive classroom work with individualized field placements and research opportunities in grassroots development and social change projects in rural and urban settings alike. MSID offers programs in Ecuador, India, Kenya, and Senegal, with two enrollment options at each site—academic year and fall semester only. Participants study international development theory, cross-cultural communication, history and culture, and local language during the first portion of fall semester. The classroom period is followed by a field placement which serves as a laboratory for the concepts and theories discussed in the classroom. Typical categories for field placements and internships include public health, education, environmental protection, social services, and agriculture.

Mobility International USA

PO Box 10767, Eugene, OR 97440
or
45 West Broadway, Suite 202, Eugene, OR 97401
Tel: (541) 343-1284 (voice/TTY) Fax: (541) 343-6812
E-mail: info@miusa.org   Website: www.miusa.org

꒡ Mobility International USA's (MIUSA) international exchanges specialize in leadership training, community service, cross-cultural experiential learning, and advocacy for the rights and inclusion of people with disabilities. These short term group exchanges for youth, adults, and professionals with and without disabilities take place in the United States and abroad. MIUSA has coordinated exchanges with Azerbaijan, Bulgaria, China, Costa Rica, East Asia, Germany, Italy, Japan, Mexico, Russia, the United Kingdom, and other countries. Activities include training seminars and workshops, adaptive recreational activities, cross-cultural communication, language classes, and volunteer service projects. Exchanges vary from ten days to three weeks in length.

MIUSA's National Clearinghouse on Disability and Exchange (NCDE) provides additional information on international exchange, volunteer, and community service opportunities. NCDE staff can respond to inquiries on the range of opportunities available and on how people with disabilities can make these possibilities a reality.

Nicaragua Network
(See listing under International Voluntary Service Organizations)

Our Developing World
13004 Paseo Presada, Saratoga, CA 95070-4125
Tel: (408) 379-4431   Fax: (408) 376-0755
E-mail: odw@magiclink.net

꒡ The main focus of Our Developing World (ODW) is to bring the realities of the Third World and the richness of diverse cultures to North Americans through programs in schools, churches, and community groups. Once a year, ODW leads study tours. Past destinations have included Cuba, Nicaragua,

Honduras, Mozambique, Zimbabwe, South Africa, the Philippines, Vietnam, Cambodia, Laos, and Hawaii. The tours provide an opportunity to talk with peasants, workers, women's associations, health workers, and co-op members, as well as a chance to learn about health, agrarian reform, human rights and educational campaigns, and economic and social planning.

Plowshares Institute

PO Box 243, Simsbury, CT 06070
Tel: (860) 651-4304   Fax: (860) 651-4305
E-mail: plowshares@hartsem.edu
Website: www.plowsharesinstitute.com

✍ Plowshares tours initiate cross-cultural dialogue between peoples of developed and developing nations. Participants commit to both advance preparation and community education work upon their return. Trip itineraries include meetings with religious and civic leaders, homestay experiences, and visits to development projects. The Institute plans two- to three-week programs to South America, Africa, South and Southeast Asia, Australia, and the South Pacific.

Quaker Workcamps International

1225 Geranium Street NW, Washington, DC 20012
Tel: (202) 722-1461   Fax: (202) 723-5376
E-mail: hjconferqwi@igc.org   Website: www.quaker.org/qwi

✍ Quaker Workcamps International offers a volunteer program for rebuilding burned churches around the US. Volunteers pay their own transportation plus a fee of $150 per week to cover room, board, and activities. Scholarships are available.

School for International Training

SIT Grassroots Development and NGO Management Program

GIIM Admissions
Kipling Road, PO Box 676, Brattleboro, VT 05302-0676
Tel: (800) 336-1616 or (802) 257-7751   Fax: (802) 258-3248
E-mail: info@sit.edu   Website: www.sit.edu
⤷ The Organization of Rural Associations for Progress
(ORAP) in Bulawayo, Zimbabwe and the School for
International Training (SIT) in Vermont combine their resources
to educate development workers and leaders from both Africa
and the US. The certificate program, based in Zimbabwe, is
open to middle-level staff of African nongovernmental organizations and to highly prepared undergraduate students and recent
graduates from US colleges and universities. Students alternate
between full group instruction at the ORAP complex in
Bulawayo and small group and individual assignments in the
villages where ORAP and other participating NGOs are
working.

The Sokoni Safari
Bridges to Community
PO Box 35, Scarborough, New York, NY 10510
Tel: (914) 923-2200
and
International Communities for the Renewal of the Earth
PO Box 194, Cross River, NY 10518
Tel: (914) 763-5790 or (415) 648-0908
⤷ The Sokoni Safari, a joint project of Bridges to Community
and International Communities for the Renewal of the Earth,
is a two-week trip to Kenya organized and managed largely by
the staff of the Greenbelt Movement, one of East Africa's fore-
most environmental organizations. Participants will stay with
Greenbelt at their Nairobi headquarters, learning about its
work and about Kenyan culture and politics. We will also travel

to rural Kenya, staying with families in a village and assisting
with agricultural tasks. Throughout the tour, participants will
examine cultural differences and the relationship between Third
World poverty and First World lending institutions, consumer
markets, and lifestyles.

Cost of the fourteen-day journey is $2,000 per person plus
airfare, $1,500 per person plus airfare for students. Limited
partial scholarships are available. Fee includes accommodations,
meals, internal travel, and a contribution to the Greenbelt
Movement. Contact any of the above phone numbers for further information and reservations.

Third World Opportunities Program
1363 Sommermont Drive, El Cajon, CA 92021
Tel/Fax: (619) 449-9381
E-mail: pgray@ucsd.edu
🖋 The Third World Opportunities Program (TWO) is a hunger
and poverty awareness program designed to provide opportunities for appropriate responses to human need. It seeks to
encourage sensitivity to life in the Third World; intentional
reflection on our relationship with Third World people; effective
work projects that offer practical services to the hungry, homeless, and the poor; and organized efforts to change existing
conditions. TWO offers a two-pronged program consisting of
an awareness tour along the US/Mexico border followed by a
short-term work project such as a six-day service assignment at
orphanages in Tecate and Las Palmas, Mexico.

Unitarian Universalist Service Committee
130 Prospect Street, Cambridge, MA 02139-1845
Tel: (617) 868-6600   Fax: (617) 868-7102
E-mail: postmaster@uusc.org   Website: www.uusc.org

🌱 The Unitarian Universalist Service Committee (UUSC) works in partnership with grassroots organizations in the United States and overseas to confront many different forms of oppression. UUSC sponsors short term work camps in locations around the US. In 2000, construction and/or renovation projects took place on Native reservations in South Dakota and Arizona, in African-American neighborhoods in Tennessee, and in a migrant farm worker community in the state of Washington. Camps run from a few days to a few weeks. Volunteers are self-funded and live in safe and simple accommodations with meals provided. Participants have ranged in age from 16 to 81; special camps for youth are available.

US Servas

11 John Street, #407, New York, NY 10038
Tel: (212) 267-0252
E-mail: usservas@servas.org   Website: www.servas.org
🌱 Servas is an international cooperative system of hosts and travelers established to help build world peace by providing opportunities for personal contact among people of diverse cultures and backgrounds. Travelers are invited to share life in the home and community and their concerns about social and international problems for short term two-night stays. Some hosts offer longer visits. Membership application for travelers consists of an interview, two character references, and a $65 membership fee per adult. Prospective hosts must also be inter-viewed and fill out an application. To receive an application, send a SASE or visit the website to download one.

Venceremos Brigade

PO Box 7071, Oakland, CA 94601

Tel: (415) 267-0606

Email: info@vbrigade.org   Website: www.vbrigade.org

☙ Venceremos Brigade participants travel for up to two weeks in Cuba, visit schools, factories, clinics, and hospitals; have informal visits and discussions with Cubans; and participate in educational seminars with representatives from other countries. Brigade members participate in workcamp activities. Each participant must be at least 18 years old, be a US citizen and have a valid passport, and not currently in the military service. Upon acceptance, participants attend a required series of preparatory sessions and commit to work in some aspect of Brigade education projects upon return. They are expected to pay transportation and miscellaneous expenses. Brigade committees are located in various areas throughout the US.

Voices on the Border Educational Delegations
1600 Webster Street NE, Washington, DC 20017

Tel: (202) 529-2912   ·   Fax: (202) 529-0897

E-mail: voices@igc.org

☙ Voices on the Border promotes contact between the repatriated communities in eastern El Salvador and interested individuals in the US through delegations to these communities. Delegations generally last for ten days and take place several times a year. Total cost of participating is approximately $1,000 plus airfare.

WWOOF International
(Willing Workers on Organic Farms)
PO Box 2675, Lewes BN7 1RB, ENGLAND

Website: www.wwoof.org

Website has e-mail contact page

♪ WWOOF International (Willing Workers on Organic Farms)
provides those who would like to volunteer on organic farms
with a list of host farms throughout the world. The purpose of
WWOOF is to enable people to learn firsthand about organic
growing techniques, expose urban dwellers to farm life and
work, and help farmers make organic production a viable alter-
native. WWOOF organizations exist in many countries, and
WWOOF host farms exist even in countries without a
WWOOF headquarters. Among the nations represented are
Brazil, Cambodia, Chile, Costa Rica, Ecuador, Ghana, India,
Ivory Coast, Malaysia, Sri Lanka, and Togo, as well as several
European countries, Australia, and New Zealand. If you would
like to volunteer in a given country, contact the country's
WWOOF organization; if there isn't one, contact WWOOF
International in the United Kingdom, either through its website
or by writing to the above address and enclosing a SASE and an
international reply coupon, available at any post office. A list of
national WWOOF organizations can be found on the website.

Farm opportunities vary in the amount of skill or experience expected, but many hosts require none. Room and board
are provided at all sites. Volunteers should keep in mind that
WWOOF is merely a contact service. It provides the address of
the farm but the volunteer must work out the placement with
the host and obtain any necessary visas and work permits.

RESOURCES

Other Organizations

THESE GROUPS DO not generally sponsor intern or travel programs—they distribute information about volunteer or travel opportunities, foreign countries, underrepresented cultures, or aspects of development.

Alternative Opportunities Clearinghouse

JustAct, 333 Valencia Street, Suite 101, San Francisco, CA 94103

Tel: (415) 431-4204 Fax: (415) 431-5953

E-mail: info@justact.org Website: www.justact.org

❧ JustAct: Youth Action for Global Justice works to develop in young people a lifelong commitment to social and economic justice around the world. JustAct's Alternative Opportunities Clearinghouse is a research and referral service for those seeking to volunteer in the United States or abroad. Potential volunteers indicate skills and interests by questionnaire and receive information on volunteer and internship programs that match their needs. A manual search with results returned by mail is $30; the online search is free. Most users of the service are 18 to 25 years of age, but there is no upper age limit. Included in the service are current materials and applications for matched organizations, JustAct's Guide to Fundraising for Grassroots Development, and advice sheets with tips on fundraising, preparing for your trip, and planning your return. JustAct also offers educational readers on current global issues.

Bank Information Center (BIC)

733 15th Street NW, Suite 1126, Washington, DC 20005

Tel: (202) 737-7752   Fax: (202) 737-1155

E-mail: info@bicusa.org   Website: www.bicusa.org

➮ Provides hard-to-obtain information on the projects and policies of multilateral development banks (like the World Bank) to environmental and social justice organizations in developing countries. Offers numerous publications and reports and advocates for greater transparency in World Bank operations. There is much documentation here of the processes by which development is managed and mismanaged.

Center for Civil Society International (CCSI)

2929 NE Blakeley Street, Seattle, WA 98105

Tel: (206) 523-4755   Fax: (206) 523-1974

E-mail: ccsi@u.washington.edu

Website: www.friends-partners.org/~ccsi

➮ Private nonpartisan educational organization promoting ideas and information for civic action worldwide. Publishes many books with a focus on the former Soviet Union.

CIVICUS: World Alliance for Citizen Participation

US Office, 919 18th Street NW, 3rd Floor, Washington, DC 20006

Tel: (202) 331-8518   Fax: (202) 331-8774

E-mail: info@civicus.org   Website: www.civicus.org

➮ An international alliance dedicated to strengthening citizen action and civil society throughout the world, especially in areas where participatory democracy and freedom of citizen association are threatened. The website contains links to its multitude of membership NGOs. Publishes books and a bimonthly newsletter following trends and offering analyses

on the third sector movement worldwide. Its atlas, available
free online as well as in other formats, profiles the state
of civil society in dozens of countries—size and scope,
economic impact, legal and tax framework, state of relations
with government and business sectors, and names of resource
organizations. The theme for its international conference in
August 2001 will be "Putting the Citizen at the Center:
Strengthening Voluntarism and Participatory Democracy."

Center for Community Change (CCC)

1000 Wisconsin Avenue NW, Washington, DC 20007

Tel: (202) 342-0567

West Coast office:

160 Sansome Street, 7th Floor, San Francisco, CA 94104

Tel: (415) 982-0346

E-mail: info@communitychange.org

Website: www.communitychange.org

🖋 For almost thirty years, the Center for Community Change
has helped grassroots organizations build their communities'
capacity for self-help by training community organizers and
providing technical assistance to community organizations.
Website contains information on aspects of poverty in the
US—including housing, jobs, transportation, health, and policy—and profiles of advocacy projects with which CCC has
assisted. Site also includes downloadable reports, the online
newsletter *Organizing* (focusing on the welfare reform debate),
policy alerts, facts and figures on wealth distribution, a list of
groups besides CCC that train community organizers, and
brochures aimed at grassroots groups with titles such as
"How to Lobby Without Regrets" and "Get Me to the Polls
On Time."

Council on International Educational Exchange (CIEE)

205 East 42nd Street, New York, NY 10017-5706

Tel: (800) 2COUNCIL or (212) 822-2600   Fax: (212) 822-2699

Website: www.ciee.org

⋗ Offers a range of study abroad, travel, volunteer, and internship programs for youth, college students, recent graduates, and teachers. Also maintains a database of job listings abroad.

Cultural Survival, Inc.

221 Prospect Street, Cambridge, MA 02139

Tel: (617) 441-5400   Fax: (617) 441-5417

E-mail: csinc@cs.org   Website: www.cs.org

⋗ Promotes the cause of self-determination for indigenous peoples worldwide. Provides organizational support and fiscal sponsorship for projects in indigenous communities, and publishes reports on a host of topics relating to development.

Doctors for Global Health (DGH)

Box 1761, Decatur, GA 30031   Tel/Fax (404) 377-3566

E-mail: ccs-dgh@ix.netcom.com Website: www.dghonline.org

⋗ Sponsors health and human rights work around the globe.

Focus on the Global South (FOCUS)

c/o CUSRI, Chulalongkorn University, Bangkok 10330 THAILAND

E-mail: admin@focusweb.org   Website: www.focusweb.org

⋗ Supports a program of progressive development policy research and practice, dedicated to regional and global policy analysis and advocacy work. Its emphasis is on the developing nations of the southern hemisphere, particularly the Asia-Pacific region. Many of its articles and reports are available online.

Fund for Reconciliation and Development (FRD)
475 Riverside Drive, Suite 727, New York, NY 10115
Tel: (212) 367-4220   Fax: (212) 367-4366
E-mail: usindo@igc.org   Website: www.usirp.org
🍂 Promotes cooperation between US nonprofit organizations
and their counterparts in Vietnam, Laos, Cambodia, and Cuba.
FRD organizes conferences in the United States and publishes
a quarterly newsletter, *Interchange*.

Grassroots International
179 Boylston Street, 4th Floor, Boston, MA 02130
Tel: (617) 524-1400   Fax: (617) 524-5525
Website: www.grassrootsonline.org
🍂 Through cash grants and material aid, Grassroots
International supports the work of NGOs in Haiti, Mexico,
Brazil, Eritrea, Palestine, and East Timor. Performs education
and advocacy on a range of issues.

**Institute for Transportation and Development Policy
(ITDP)**
115 West 30th Street, Suite 1205, New York, NY 10001
Tel: (212) 629-8001
E-mail: mobility@igc.org   Website: www.itdp.org
🍂 Focuses on the potential of non-motorized transportation in
alleviating poverty. Aimed at changing policies of international
lending agencies. Provides technical assistance about how to
incorporate non-motorized transportation into development
projects.

InterAction: American Council for Voluntary Action
1717 Massachusetts Avenue NW, Suite 701, Washington, DC 20036
Tel: (202) 667-8227   Fax: (202) 667-8236

E-mail: publications@interaction.org
Website: www.interaction.org
🌶 The United States' largest coalition of nonprofits working on sustainable development, refugee and disaster assistance, and humanitarian aid. Publishes *Monday Developments*, a bi-weekly newsletter covering news and commentary on the international NGO scene and listing job opportunities at various organizations, and *Member Profiles*, an annual directory of their member nonprofits, as well as Country Situation and Member Activities reports.

International Development Exchange (IDEX)
827 Valencia Street, Suite 101, San Francisco, CA 94110
Tel: (415) 824-8384
E-mail: idex@idex.org   Website: www.idex.org
🌶 Supports community-based development efforts in Africa, Asia, and Latin America and engages US citizens in educational partnerships with these communities.

The International Ecotourism Society (TIES)
PO Box 668, Burlington, VT 05402
Tel: (802) 651-9818   Fax: (802) 651-9819
E-mail: ecomail@ecotourism.org Website: www.ecotourism.org
🌶 An international membership organization dedicated to disseminating information about ecologically-sound and sustainable tourism. Individual memberships are $35 per year, and include subscription to newsletter, discounts on TIES publications, and access to lists of tour and lodge operators.

International Volunteer Programs Association (IVPA)
1221 Preservation Park Way, #100, Oakland, CA 94612
Tel: (510) 763-9206   Fax: (510) 763-9290

Website: www.volunteerinternational.org

꘍ The International Volunteer Programs Association is an alliance of nonprofit nongovernmental organizations based in the Americas that are involved in international volunteer and internship exchanges. IVPA's website has a database of volunteer opportunities as well as general advice on fundraising and traveling abroad.

Mexico Solidarity Network

1247 E Street SE, Washington, DC 20003

Tel: (202) 544-9355

E-mail: msn@mexicosolidarity.org

Website: www.mexicosolidarity.org

꘍ Mexico Solidarity Network (MSN) is a coalition of over 75 US organizations supporting justice and democracy in Mexico, with special attention to the indigenous population of Chiapas. Provides up-to-the-minute information on the Mexican political situation and can put you in touch with groups sponsoring delegations to the area.

Panos Institute (PI)

1701 K Street NW, Suite 1100, Washington, DC 20006

Tel: (202) 223-7949   Fax: (202) 223-7947

E-mail: panos@cais.com

Website: www.panosinst.org or www.panos.org.uk

꘍ The Panos Institute specializes in news and research about development issues, and aims to stimulate public debate by providing accessible information on neglected or poorly-understood topics as they affect the developing world, particularly in the fields of poverty, gender, environment, reproductive health, and population. PI publishes books, feature articles, briefings, and collected oral testimonies.

The Rethinking Tourism Project

PO Box 581938, Minneapolis, MN 55458-1938

Tel: (651) 644-9984

🍂 Works with indigenous communities to develop critical educational materials and information-sharing on a wide range of tourism-related subjects—human rights, displacement, migration, policy, education, and others.

SANGONet

Tel: 011-27-11-838-6943   Fax: 011-27-492-1058

E-mail: info@sn.apc.org   Website: www.sangonet.org.za

🍂 Based in Johannesburg, SANGONet, Southern Africa's nonprofit internet service provider, is a regional electronic communications network for development and human rights workers. It delivers relevant information to people working in development and aims to build capacity in organizations through the use of electronic communication. Site contains information and links organized by topic from the Southern Africa NGO world.

Youth Action for Peace (YAP)

International Secretariat

Avenue du Parc Royal 3, B-1020 Brussels, BELGIUM

Tel: 32-2-478-94-10   Fax: 32-2-478-94-32

E-mail: yapis@xs4all.be   Website: www.yap.org

🍂 Founded in 1923 under the name Christian Movement for Peace, YAP is an international youth organization working to end war and social exclusion through volunteer exchanges and peace and development education. YAP has no US branch but provides extensive opportunity listings, a newsletter, and links on its website.

Guides to International Voluntary Service

How to Live Your Dream of Volunteering Overseas. Joseph Collins, Stefano DeZerega, and Zahara Heckscher (New York: Viking Penguin, 2001).

The International Directory of Voluntary Work (Oxford, UK: Vacation-Work, 1997). Distributed in the United States by Peterson's Guides, PO Box 67005, Lawrenceville, NJ 08648, Tel: (800) 338-3282.

International Directory of Youth Internships: With the United Nations, Its Specialized Agencies, and Non-Governmental Organizations, Michael Culligan and Cynthia T. Morehouse, eds. (New York: Apex Press, 1994). The Apex Press, PO Box 337, Croton-on-Hudson, NY 10520, Tel: (800) 316-APEX or (914) 271-6500.

International Internships and Volunteer Programs and International Options for Students and Professionals, Will Cantrell and Francine Modderno (Oakton, VA: Worldwise Books, 1992). Worldwise Books, PO Box 3030, Oakton, VA 22124, Tel: (703) 620-1972.

The Peace Corps and More: 175 Ways to Work, Study and Travel in the Third World (Santa Ana, CA: Seven Locks Press, 1997). Available from Global Exchange, 2017 Mission Street, Suite 303, San Francisco, CA 94110, Tel: (415) 255-7296.

Social Change Through Voluntary Action, M. L. Dantwala, et al. (Thousand Oaks, CA: Sage Publications, Inc., 1998). Sage

Publications, Inc., 2455 Teller Road, Thousand Oaks, CA
91320, Tel: (805) 499-0721.

*Volunteer Work: A Comprehensive Guide to Medium and Long-
Term Voluntary Service 1993,* Hilary Sewell (London, UK:
Kuperard Limited, 1993). Distributed in the US by Seven Hills
Book Distributors, 1531 Tremont Street, Cincinnati, OH
45214, Tel: (800) 545-2005.

Working for Global Justice Directory (San Francisco, CA:
JustAct, 1999). JustAct, 333 Valencia Street, Suite 110, San
Francisco, CA 94103, Tel: (415) 431-4204.

Work, Study, Travel Abroad: The Whole World Handbook,
Council on International Educational Exchange (CIEE). (New
York: CIEE Publications, 1995). Out of print, but worth trying
to find used or in a library.

Guides to US Voluntary Service

Internships 1998 (Lawrenceville, NJ: Peterson's Guides, 1998).
Peterson's Guides, PO Box 67005, Lawrenceville, NJ 08648,
Tel: (800) 338-3282.

*Volunteer! The Comprehensive Guide to Voluntary Service in
the US and Abroad 1995,* Council on International Educational
Exchange (New York: CIEE Publications, 1995) Out of print,
but worth trying to find used or in a library.

*A World of Options for the 90s: Guide to International
Educational Exchange and Travel for Persons with*

Disabilities (Eugene, OR: Mobility International, 1997)
Mobility International USA, PO Box 10760, Eugene, OR
97440, Tel: (503) 343-1284.

Guides to Study Overseas

*Financial Resources for International Study: A Guide for US
Nationals,* Sara Steen, ed. (New York: Institute of International
Education, 1996). Institute of International Education, 809
United Nations Plaza, New York, NY 10017, Tel: (800) 445-
0443 or (301) 617-7804.

International Studies Funding and Resources Book (Croton-
on-Hudson, NY: Apex Press, 1990) The Apex Press, PO Box
337, Croton-on-Hudson, NY 10520, Tel: (800) 316-APEX or
(914) 271-6500.

*Smart Vacations: The Travelers' Guide to Learning Adventures
Abroad,* Priscilla Tovey, ed. (New York: St. Martin's Press, 1993).

Publications on Travel and Tourism

Whether you intend to travel or volunteer abroad, the higher-
quality tourist guides can provide background on the history,
political situation, customs, and culture of countries or regions
which interest you. Check the travel section of your local book-
store or contact the publishers of the series below:

Lonely Planet Publications, Lonely Planet USA
Embarcadero West, 150 Linden Street, Oakland, CA 94607-2538

Tel: (800) 275-8555 or (510) 893-8555   Fax: (510) 893-8563
E-mail: info@lonelyplanet.com   Website: www.lonelyplanet.com
🌿 Lonely Planet has an especially rich and detailed website,
featuring bulletin boards, e-mail discussions, and up-to-the-
minute information on numerous countries.

Moon Travel Handbooks (covering the Americas, Asia, and the Pacific)
Avalon Travel Publishing
5855 Beaudry Street, Emeryville, CA 94608
Tel: (510) 595-3664
E-mail: travel@moon.com   Website: www.moon.com

Rough Guides USA
345 Hudson Street, New York, NY 10014
Tel: (212) 414-3635
Website: www.roughguides.com

*Alternative Travel Directory: The Complete Guide to Traveling,
Studying, and Living Overseas, sixth edition*, Nicole Rosenleaf
Ritter and Clayton A. Hubbs, eds. (Amherst, MA: Transitions
Abroad Publishing, Inc., 2000). Transitions Abroad Publishing,
Inc., PO Box 1300, Amherst, MA 01004-1300.

*Fodor's Great American Learning Vacations, 1997, second
edition* (New York: Fodor's Travel Publications, 1997). Random
House, 1540 Broadway, New York, NY 10036.

Free Vacations and Bargain Adventures in the USA, Evelyn
Kaye (Boulder, CO: Blue Panda Publications, 1998). Blue Panda
Publications, 3031 Fifth Street, Boulder, Colorado 80304.

*Rethinking Tourism and Ecotravel: The Paving of Paradise
and What You Can Do to Stop It,* Deborah McLaren (West
Hartford, CT: Kumarian Press, 1998). Kumarian Press, 14
Oakwood Avenue, West Hartford, CT 06119, Tel: (800) 289-
2664 or (860) 233-5895.

Transitions Abroad. Transitions Abroad Publishing, Inc., PO
Box 1300, Amherst, MA 01004-1300. A bimonthly publication.

*Volunteer Vacations: Directory of Short Term Adventures That
Will Benefit You and Others, seventh edition,* Bill McMillon
(Chicago, IL: Chicago Review Press, 1999). Chicago Review
Press, 814 North Franklin, Chicago, IL 60610.

Resources For Finding Jobs In Development

ACCESS: Networking in the Public Interest
1001 Connecticut Avenue NW, Suite 838, Washington, DC 20036
Tel: (202) 785-4233
Website: www.communityjobs.org
🖋 Lists employment and internship opportunities in the
nonprofit sector on its website. Sponsors career fairs in
locations around the country.

Careers In International Affairs, sixth edition, School of
Foreign Service (Washington, DC: Georgetown University
Press, 1996). Georgetown University Press, Georgetown
University, Washington, DC 20057, Tel: (800) 246-9606.

International Career Employment Weekly
and International Employment Hotline (monthly)
International Career Employment Center
Carlyle Corporation
1088 Middle River Road, Stanardsville, VA 22973
Tel: (804) 985-6444   Fax: (804) 985-6828
E-mail: Lisa@internationaljobs.org
Website: www.internationaljobs.org
❧ Both publications contain extensive overseas job listings in
the public and private sectors. Orientation is toward skilled
professionals. The Center also publishes an annual guide to
overseas internships.

Job Opportunities Bulletin. Director of Recruitment,
Transcentury Foundation, 1724 Kalorama Road NW,
Washington, DC 20009, Tel: (202) 328-4424
❧ Bi-monthly publication.

Working for Global Justice Directory
(San Francisco, CA: JustAct, 1999)
JustAct, 333 Valencia Street, Suite 110, San Francisco, CA 94103
Tel: (415) 431-4204

Online Resources

Association of Voluntary Service Organizations
Website: www.avso.org
❧ Association of national and international nonprofits based in
Europe. Site contains volunteer opportunities, links, and bul-
letin board.

Grass-roots.org

Website: www.grass-roots.org

꙳ Lively descriptions of over 200 grassroots organizations in
the United States working in diverse and often innovative ways
to eliminate poverty. Robin Garr, creator of the website, has
also authored a book, *Reinvesting in America*, with many more
program descriptions, along with a "Getting Involved" appendix
list of groups that need volunteers.

Idealist (a project of Action Without Borders)

Website: www.idealist.org

꙳ Lists thousands of volunteer opportunities and nonprofit
jobs; offers publications and resources for nonprofits and
consultants.

Project Cooperating for Cooperation

Website: www.coop4coop.org

꙳ Comprehensive directory of development organizations and
volunteer programs. Under construction as of mid-2000, but
promising.

INDEX TO ORGANIZATIONS

fOOD fIRST BOOKS Of
RELATED INTEREST

America Needs Human Rights
Edited by Anuradha Mittal and Peter Rosset
   This new anthology includes writings on understanding human rights, poverty in America, and welfare reform and human rights.   Paperback, $13.95

Views from the South: The Effects of Globalization and the WTO on Third World Countries
Foreword by Jerry Mander
Afterword by Anuradha Mittal
Edited by Sarah Anderson
   This rare collection of essays by Third World activists and scholars describes in pointed detail the effects of the WTO and other Bretton Woods institutions.
   Paperback $12.95

The Paradox of Plenty: Hunger in a Bountiful World
Edited by Douglas H. Boucher
   Excerpts from Food First's best writings on world hunger and what we can do to change it.   Paperback, $18.95

Basta! Land and the Zapatista Rebellion in Chiapas
Revised edition
George A. Collier with Elizabeth Lowery Quaratiello
Foreword by Peter Rosset
   The classic on the Zapatista in a new revised edition, including a preface by Roldolfo Stavenhagen, a new epilogue about

the present challenges to the indigenous movement in Chiapas, and an updated bibliography.   Paperback, $14.95

Benedita da Silva:
An Afro-Brazilian Woman's Story of Politics and Love
As told to Medea Benjamin and Maisa Mendonça
Foreword by Jesse Jackson

Afro-Brazilian Senator Benedita da Silva shares the inspiring story of her life as an advocate for the rights of women and the poor.   Paperback, $15.95

Breakfast of Biodiversity: The Truth about
Rain Forest Destruction
John Vandermeer and Ivette Perfecto

Analyzes deforestation from both an environmental and social justice perspective.   Paperback, $16.95

Education for Action: Graduate Studies
with a Focus on Social Change
Third edition
Edited by Sean Brooks and Alison Knowles

An authoritative, easy-to-use guidebook that provides information on progressive programs in a wide variety of fields.
Paperback, $8.95.

Kerala: Radical Reform as Development in an Indian State
Revised edition
Richard W. Franke and Barbara H. Chasin

In the last eighty years, the Indian state of Kerala has experimented in the use of radical reform that has brought it some of the Third World's highest levels of health, education, and social justice.   Paperback, $10.95

Needless Hunger: Voices from a Bangladesh Village
James Boyce and Betsy Hartmann

The global analysis of Food First is vividly captured here in a single village.   Paperback, $6.95

Video: The Greening of Cuba
Directed by Jaime Kibben

Cuba has combined time-tested traditional methods with cutting edge bio-technology, reminding us that developed and developing nations can choose a healthier environment and still feed their people.   VHS videotape, $29.95.

Write or call our distributor to place book orders. All orders must be pre-paid. Please add $4.50 for the first book and $1.50 for each additional book for shipping and handling.

LPC Group
1436 West Randolph Street
Chicago, IL 60607
(800) 243-0138
www.coolbooks.com

ABOUT FOOD FIRST

(Institute for Food and Development Policy)

Food First, also known as the Institute for Food and Development Policy, is a nonprofit research and education-for-action center dedicated to investigating and exposing the root causes of hunger in a world of plenty. It was founded in 1975 by Frances Moore Lappé, author of the bestseller *Diet for a Small Planet*, and food policy analyst Dr. Joseph Collins. Food First research has revealed that hunger is created by concentrated economic and political power, not by scarcity. Resources and decision-making are in the hands of a wealthy few, depriving the majority of land, jobs, and therefore food.

Hailed by *The New York Times* as "one of the most established food think tanks in the country," Food First has grown to profoundly shape the debate about hunger and development.

But Food First is more than a think tank. Through books, reports, videos, media appearances, and speaking engagements, Food First experts not only reveal the often hidden roots of hunger, they show how individuals can get involved in bringing an end to the problem. Food First inspires action by bringing to light the courageous efforts of people around the world who are creating farming and food systems that truly meet people's needs.

HOW TO BECOME A MEMBER OR
INTERN OF FOOD FIRST

Become a Member of Food First

Private contributions and membership gifts form the financial
base of Food First/Institute for Food and Development Policy.
The success of the Institute's programs depends not only on its
dedicated volunteers and staff, but on financial activists as well.
Each member strengthens Food First's efforts to change a hungry
world. We invite you to join Food First. As a member you will
receive a twenty percent discount on all Food First books. You
will also receive our quarterly publication, *Food First News and
Views*, and timely *Backgrounders* that provide information and
suggestions for action on current food and hunger crises in the
United States and around the world. If you want so subscribe to
our internet newsletter, *Food RightsWatch*, send us an e-mail at
foodfirst@foodfirst.org. All contributions are tax-deductible.

Become an Intern for Food First

There are opportunities for interns in research, advocacy, cam-
paigning, publishing, computers, media, and publicity at Food
First. Our interns come from around the world. They are a vital
part of our organization and make our work possible.

To become a member or apply to become an intern, just call,
visit our web site, or clip and return the attached coupon to

Food First/Institute for Food and Development Policy

398 60th Street, Oakland, CA 94618, USA
Phone: (510) 654-4400   Fax: (510) 654-4551
E-mail: foodfirst@foodfirst.org   Web site: www.foodfirst.org

You are also invited to give a gift membership to others interested
in the fight to end hunger.

JOINING FOOD FIRST

☐ I want to join Food First and receive a 20% discount
on this and all subsequent orders. Enclosed
is my tax-deductible contribution of:

☐ $30   ☐ $50   ☐ $100   ☐ $500   ☐ $1,000   ☐ Other

NAME _____

ADDRESS _____

CITY/STATE/ZIP _____

DAYTIME PHONE (_____) _____

E-MAIL _____

ORDERING FOOD FIRST MATERIALS

ITEM DESCRIPTION	QTY	UNIT COST	TOTAL

PAYMENT METHOD:

☐ CHECK

☐ MONEY ORDER

☐ MASTERCARD

☐ VISA

MEMBER DISCOUNT, 20%	$_____
CA RESIDENTS SALES TAX 8.25%	$_____
SUBTOTAL	$_____
POSTAGE: 15% UPS: 20% ($2 MIN.)	$_____
MEMBERSHIP(S)	$_____
ADDITIONAL CONTRIBUTION	$_____
TOTAL ENCLOSED	$_____

_____
NAME ON CARD

_____
CARD NUMBER   EXP. DATE

_____
SIGNATURE

MAKE CHECK OR MONEY ORDER PAYABLE TO:

Food First, 398 - 60th Street, Oakland, CA 94618

FOOD FIRST GIFT BOOKS

Please send a Gift Book to (order form on reverse side):

NAME _____

ADDRESS _____

CITY/STATE/ZIP _____

FROM: _____

FOOD FIRST PUBLICATIONS CATALOGS

Please send a Publications Catalog to:

NAME _____

ADDRESS _____

CITY/STATE/ZIP _____

NAME _____

ADDRESS _____

CITY/STATE/ZIP _____

NAME _____

ADDRESS _____

CITY/STATE/ZIP _____

FOOD FIRST GIFT MEMBERSHIPS

☐ Enclosed is my tax-deductible contribution of:

☐ $30   ☐ $50   ☐ $100   ☐ $500   ☐ $1,000   ☐ Other

Please send a Food First membership to:

NAME _____

ADDRESS _____

CITY/STATE/ZIP _____

FROM: _____